Listening and Spiritual Conversation

Sue Pickering is an Anglican priest, spiritual director and supervisor in New Zealand. Involved at a national level in the training of spiritual directors, Sue is currently a Canon of Taranaki Cathedral Church, New Plymouth, and leads workshops on spirituality and ageing.

Also by the same author and available from Canterbury Press:

Creative Ideas for Quiet Days: Resources and Liturgies for Retreats and Days of Reflection
With CD Rom
'a veritable feast ... a treasury of ideas and encouragement'
Margaret Silf

Spiritual Direction: A Practical Introduction
'This is quite simply the book on spiritual direction we've been waiting on for years.'
Gordon Jeff

Creative Retreat Ideas: Resources for Short, Day and Weekend Retreats
'An excellent book. Highly recommended.'
The Good Bookstall

On Holiday with God
'An outstanding guide for any Christian contemplating a self-directed retreat.'
Presence

Creative Ideas for Ministry with the Aged
'A book of resources which offers exceptional riches.'
Church Times

Listening and Spiritual Conversation

Singing God-songs in a noisy world

Sue Pickering

CANTERBURY
PRESS
Norwich

First published in 2017 by the Canterbury Press Norwich
Editorial office
3rd Floor, Invicta House
108–114 Golden Lane
London EC1Y 0TG, UK

Canterbury Press is an imprint of Hymns Ancient & Modern Ltd
(a registered charity)

Hymns Ancient & Modern

Hymns Ancient & Modern® is a registered trademark of Hymns Ancient & Modern Ltd
13A Hellesdon Park Road, Norwich,
Norfolk NR6 5DR, UK

www.canterburypress.co.uk

British Library Cataloguing in Publication data

A catalogue record for this book is available
from the British Library

978 1 84825 910 2

Printed and bound in Great Britain by
Ashford Colour Press Ltd

Contents

Acknowledgements

Writing a book is a bit like having a baby, except this one took two years, not nine months! I am truly grateful to those who've accompanied me during this protracted gestation: those with whom I've shared Monday morning prayers (Con, Ros, David, Jen and Peter) and Tuesday morning Eucharists (++Philip, Michael, David P., Ailsa, Helene, Titia, Con, Jenny, Donna, Gloria, David W. and Jan); those who've asked me about progress and listened kindly (Mary, Prue, Maxine, Helen and Karen), those from further afield who have prayed for me (Jane and Eirene), and those who've not really understood what I was trying to write about, but supported me anyway (remaining nameless to avoid embarrassment!)

As I've thought about those who've been formative in my own discipling, I've recalled with thanksgiving people who've taken the time to provide safe contexts in which I could learn, practise skills, test ideas and know it was okay to be asking questions, pushing boundaries. At significant times on my spiritual journey, the loving support of my husband, son, daughter-in-law and wider family; the wisdom of the late Marion Cornes; the compassionate heart, encouragement and persistence of the Reverend Peter Mitchell; the network of spiritual directors in Spiritual Growth Ministries; the generosity of my diocese and the ongoing perceptive and pastoral supervision of Archbishop Philip Richardson, have been profound vehicles of God's grace in my life.

This book includes stories of people I've met over the years in the diverse working contexts of chaplaincy, parish and spiritual direction. Most of the stories belong to people who need to remain anonymous, so their names and any identifying details have been altered. Two have agreed to be named: my heartfelt thanks to David Pearce and Eirene Voon.

It's a particular pleasure to thank Christine Smith from Canterbury Press for her patience and encouragement; and her team for their diligence and commitment to quality publications. Thanks must also go to Taranaki Cathedral Director of Music Christopher Luke, who took my somewhat shakily sung chant and turned it into a musical score in record time, and to Mike Heydon for his photo of Kahurangi, which brought an unexpected focus to the way the story unfolded.

It's not just 'form' to say that above all I acknowledge the Holy Spirit – it's the simple truth. Day after day as I recovered from leaving the ministry I loved, I would struggle to begin to write; there was interruption after interruption and sometimes weeks went by with little progress. But when I had the energy, and when my prayer for inspiration was coming from the most honest place in my soul, an idea, a story, a memory, a piece of Scripture, a relevant resource would appear and clarity would return and writing would flow.

It has very much been a partnership: I the apprentice companion in the yoke, Jesus by his Spirit, the light on the Way, the Word, the inspiration. To God be the glory.

List of illustrations

The publisher and author acknowledge with thanks permission to use photographs. Wikimedia Commons images are available under a Creative Commons Attribution-ShareAlike 3.0 licence. Unattributed photographs are by the author.

p. xvii ‘Kahurangi’ by Mike Heydon, used with permission.

p. 61 Image of a mustard seed is from www.shutterstock.org.

p. 103 Mathias Grünewald, *Crucifixion*, 1512–16, from the Isenheim altarpiece, in the Musée Unterlinden, Colmar. Photo by Vincent Desjardins, https://commons.wikimedia.org/w/index.php?curid=11167283. Used with permission.

Foreword

In July 1999 I arrived at a small regional airport late on a wintery afternoon. It was a wild and stormy day. I was given the keys to a new car and pointed in the direction of Taranaki some three-hour drive away. And it was quite a drive! The storm dramatically played around me as I navigated for the very first time a twisting road that I have come to know very well.

I had been given directions to the small town of Stratford where I was to begin a retreat in the lead up to my ordination as a bishop. When I found the small retreat centre I was greeted by a gentle priest with warm eyes, a welcoming smile, who quickly put a tired pilgrim at ease.

That is when my story began to be interwoven with Sue Pickering's. The first 24 hours of this retreat was just me, Sue and God, then we were joined by Bishop David Moxon, with whom I was to share leadership in the Diocese of Waikato and Taranaki for 14 years. Sue helped us reflect on what being yoked together might mean for creative shared leadership. Finally we were joined by my family and my friend Father Peter Norris, a Roman Catholic priest who was to preach at my ordination. Sue encouraged my very young children to fly kites in the brisk Taranaki wind. Kites that allowed the fears and hopes written on them to soar equally. We felt wrapped up with care and compassion.

Sue is a wise woman of God, an experienced spiritual director and guide. She is also a practical theologian.

This book reflects her practical wisdom, experience and insight. Behind every word is a profound love for the Church and an unshakable belief that in spite of all of its frailty and brokeness, it is still the body of Christ called and empowered to work for the Kingdom.

At the heart of the book is a simple premise; that the reclamation of the vocation of the laity to share their stories of what God is doing in their lives is central to the extension of God's Kingdom, and that it is the responsibility of clergy to enable them to do so.

Also undergirding this book is an astute analysis of the context into which the Church is embedded, and a conviction that careful listening and attention to the stories of individuals, communities and whole peoples help us to discern the work of God in our midst. This careful intentional work helps us to discern the interweaving of the ongoing narrative of God's love for the world. Above all this is a realistic yet hope-filled book. A book that speaks of God's active compassion for all that God has made.

You know that the writer of this book waits on God, listens for God and discerns God. That is what makes this book so credible and so beautiful.

Archbishop Philip Richardson
New Plymouth, New Zealand

Stories …

Stories filled my life when I was little. Fairy tales and Māori myths and legends delighted my imagination; the volumes of the Arthur Mee *Children's Encyclopaedia* offered a treasure trove as well as refuge for a solitary child. But enthralling though these tales were, they lacked the relational power of live storytelling and conversation. I was still alone when I finished reading them, until, many years later, I came to the Gospel stories and Jesus came to me.

Stories are meant for sharing, for helping people connect with their own humanity and their heritage. That's what Jesus did. At the very start of his ministry, steeped in the Jewish tradition, Jesus shared the story of his personal God-connection:

> 'The Spirit of the Lord is upon me,
> because he has anointed me
> to bring good news to the poor.
> He has sent me to proclaim release to the captives
> and recovery of sight to the blind,
> to let the oppressed go free,
> to proclaim the year of the Lord's favour.'
> And he rolled up the scroll, gave it back to the attendant, and sat down. The eyes of all in the synagogue were fixed on him.
> Then he began to say to them, 'Today this scripture has been fulfilled in your hearing.'
> *Luke 4.18–21*

This story thrills me each time I read it as I imagine Jesus, in one electrifying moment, publicly claiming his unique vocation, reassuring listeners of God's loving intention towards humanity and challenging their perceptions around the expected messiah.

Sharing stories is what the early church disciples did too. Throughout the book of Acts, the followers of the Way, convinced of the compassion, power and divinity of Jesus, tell and retell their own stories of Jesus and testify to ongoing encounters with the Holy Spirit. For example, in Acts 9—10, Ananias, acting on God's meticulous instructions, brings Saul his sight and confirms for Saul the story of his life-changing meeting with the Risen Christ on the Damascus road. Paul then shares this story wherever he goes, demonstrating, in his own actions and words, the power of God to transform. Peter speaks of his God-arranged invitation to travel to meet a Gentile named Cornelius, and sets in motion the extension of God's grace to those who had been 'outside'. And so the gospel is spread organically as more and more people speak of their experience of God's provision and presence in all the circumstances of their lives.

In any culture, alongside the telling and retelling of traditional, tribal or 'in-house' stories, new stories emerge from the life of the people. For the culture to thrive it needs both the old and the new; with singing, dancing, painting or poetry, the foundational stories of the old and the vibrancy of the new are creatively crafted into the larger story comprehensible for our times, ready for sharing age-old truths with a new generation.

But sadly, somehow, over the millennia, the dynamic process of sharing personal stories of God's activity in ordinary lives has lost momentum.

We have failed so to indwell the Gospel stories that the reality of Jesus seeps through our being and bubbles up into our daily conversation.

We have allowed ourselves to be distracted by debates, instead of committing ourselves to serving the poor and the creation.

We have struggled to notice and share the new stories of God's grace in our lives.

We have failed to love as God loves us.

Lord have mercy
Christ have mercy
Lord have mercy.

⌘

Sharing personal stories of God's activity in our lives?

Think of the story of Thomas, the disciple forever dubbed 'doubting' (John 20.24–29). For Thomas, someone else's story of an encounter with Jesus wasn't sufficient. He knew he needed his own story, his own personal God-moment for his faith to grow. Such a moment came, and with it the chance to proclaim his faith in Jesus as 'My Lord and my God!'

We often rely on other people's stories of God to get us started on our faith journeys. But for us to connect deeply with God and to be transformed into the likeness of Christ, we, like Thomas, need to know for ourselves – need to encounter God – somehow.

The eternal good news is that God is more than ready to meet us – anytime, anywhere.

That is what this book is about – learning to notice God's communication with us (becoming disciples), and learning how to share our God-story with others (becoming witnesses).

As you may have gathered, stories will naturally play a significant part in this book – the stories chosen are examples of God's interaction with people in contemporary life both within and beyond the church setting. They are all true.

My prayer is that as you read and engage with the material, there will be a holy connection between your story and God's story and that, with the precise and priceless guidance of the Holy Spirit, you will be able to share the good news God has personally written in your soul.

Let us bless the Lord!
Thanks be to God.

Kahurangi and the 'woman at the gate': two starting stories

Kahurangi

En route to a retreat a couple of years ago, I visited a rural bird sanctuary. In a large aviary lived an endangered blue-wattled kokako named Kahurangi,[1] who guarded her solitude in spite of carers' efforts to provide feathered company. Orphaned by a predator, she had been rescued and raised by human beings, but had not learned the hauntingly beautiful song that was her birthright.

However, the carer talking to our group said Kahurangi had begun to sing a few notes – maybe because carers play her species' song to her when they visit her aviary, or perhaps she's mimicking what she's heard from a pair of wild kokako defending a nearby track, or, just possibly, a male bird like 'Romeo', a kokako who courted another aviary female at the reserve some years ago, is serenading her through the wires.

Whatever the reason, it's clear that others – people or birds – are helping her discover more of what it means to be fully herself.

I was moved by her story and found myself thinking that we might describe Christian witness as singing 'our own God-songs', sharing our life experience and Jesus-stories sensitively with people we meet, particularly those deprived of their full personhood, or weighed down by concern for others.

1 'Kahurangi' has several meanings in Māori: 'blue', 'noble', 'honoured', 'a precious type of greenstone' (New Zealand jade: pounamu).

'Kahurangi' by Mike Heydon.

You may like to spend a few minutes looking closely at the picture of Kahurangi in her cage and see what comes to mind.

I asked the bird sanctuary for one of their 'professional' pictures to include in this book. When it arrived, initially I was disappointed because I had expected it to be from *my* perspective, looking at Kahurangi from *outside the wire*. But after a while, I realized that those who knew Kahurangi best were her carers, those who went into her world, spent time with her, and tried to see the world from Kahurangi's viewpoint. I saw that I needed to *change* my perspective and look at life from the other's position – a message relevant to our mission in today's world.

For those of us who have been embedded in the institutional church for decades, looking at things through an ecclesiastical lens is like a 'default setting', a fixed perspective unconsciously influencing our attitudes and practices. But when we are out and about in our neighbourhood and networks, we *cannot assume anything* about the world views of those we meet. We *don't know* what it is like to be homeless, a recently arrived immigrant from a persecuted Christian minority, a third-generation Muslim city-dweller, a woman of colour practising law in a patriarchal system, a child of the streets, a struggling student. Even if some people's situations remind us of our own story, *we are not* that person. Our experience may serve to heighten our empathy, but the person's story takes place in a distinct context with different influences.

The woman at my gate

Lara, our Labrador, began to bark suddenly. I found her on the chair looking intently out of the window. When I followed her gaze, all I could see was someone's back as he/she walked past our gate. By the time I had walked down to the pavement and looked along the road, there was no one in sight.

I decided to wait.

And then I saw her coming out of the business next door – a sari-clad woman with long, dark, grey-streaked hair. I smiled as she got nearer and she stopped and we began to talk. Beginning with comments about the weather in my country and hers, we quickly moved deeper.

I listened to her story of dislocation, disruption and concern for her family. She told me of her faith in a Hindu deity.

I said I was an Anglican priest, and asked if she'd like me to pray with her. She smiled broadly, and nodded at once.

So there on the footpath we stood, hands locked, heads almost touching as I gave her the words the Spirit brought to mind, words addressing the specific needs of those she loved, words of encouragement and hope, words of trust in God who would be active in the lives of those for whom we prayed.

'Thank you', she whispered. 'My Krishna has brought me to you.'

I spoke words of blessing in the name of Jesus.

For a moment, we stood in silence: two mothers, two women of faith. Then, after assuring her she could leave a note in my letter-box should she want to talk further, we hugged and parted.

⌘

Lara's reaction to something happening outside is more than just evidence of her naughty habit of sitting on chairs. For me it says something fundamental about the value of *looking outwards* to the life going on just beyond our gate, beyond the institutional Church.

The 'woman at my gate' story may have raised a few questions in your mind – engaging with someone from another faith for example – but fundamentally it is a story about a God-arranged connection. The woman recognized it and so did I – she needed a listening ear and prayerful support, and the Spirit worked to ensure her need was met.

Having confidence that Christ was in the conversation – in the timing, in the deepening – enabled it to unfold naturally. I continue to pray for her and her family when she comes to mind. Whether I shall ever see her again is in God's hands.

⌘

Much of the New Testament records the stories of people who were looking for support and came into contact with Jesus. In the account of the marginalized Samaritan woman at the well in John 4, we see someone so liberated by Jesus' presence, acceptance and compassionate insight that she promptly begins to sing her very new God-song, still processing her experience even as she shares it with others:

> Then the woman left her water-jar and went back to the city. She said to the people, 'Come and see a man who told me everything I have ever done! He cannot be the Messiah, can he?'
> *John 4.28–29*

And then we see the effect of her witness – the villagers are so intrigued they 'Come and see ...' for themselves, and then they *invite Jesus into their own neighbourhood*, and spend time with him. As a result of his presence and teaching among them, they begin to sing their own God-songs:

> They said to the woman, 'It is no longer because of what you said that we believe, for we have heard for ourselves, and we know that this is truly the Saviour of the world.'
> *John* 4.42

This unnamed woman, whom some call the first evangelist, offers us a model of mission born out of experience shared with integrity. She did not talk about complex theological concepts; she did not have to attend courses or jump through man-made hoops to prove she was 'in'; she *simply bore witness* to the reality of the impact of Jesus on her own life, and her experience of Jesus bubbled up to overflowing and touched her community.

As clergy, pastoral workers, family members, friends or neighbours, we cannot help others to discover and sing their unique God-song *unless* we can sing our own, unless we can express who we are in Christ, sharing our struggles and failures and the stories that reflect God's grace as we travel the transformational journey: 'renewal of our minds' and growth into 'the fullness of Christ'.
Romans 12.2; Ephesians 4.13

In his song 'He Came Singing Love', Colin Gibson[2] depicts Jesus as coming, living and dying, all the while singing his God-song of love, hope, faith and peace. But then comes the challenge:

> For the love to go on, we must make it our song.
> You and I be the singers.

There is no other way.

⌘

2 Colin Gibson, words and music © Hope Publishing Co., Carol Stream, IL, 1994. Used by permission of the composer.

This book has a practical focus, with opportunities for reflection that are designed to help you notice and celebrate the experiences and stories that make up your unique 'God-song' – how God's story interacts with your life story with all its human ups and downs. If you find some reflection questions challenging, rather than avoiding them, stop and ask God to help you attend to the feelings and thoughts that have surfaced, and be open to what God might want to say to you.

- The book can be used as a standalone resource for personal spiritual growth – along with the reflection questions there are suggestions for 'Going deeper'.
- In the 'Further reading' section at the end are resources to continue your engagement with each chapter through books, links to websites and relevant YouTube videos.
- If you think you need a refresher or some user-friendly information about the basics of the Christian faith, try exploring a simple catechism (statement of beliefs), such as that in the New Zealand Prayer Book.[3]
- The book may also be useful for spiritual friends/prayer-partners to explore together.
- If you are in leadership and seriously want to encourage your congregation in intentional discipleship and witness, I strongly recommend that you work through this book first on your own, taking the opportunity for personal reflection and 'going deeper', before sharing it with your leadership team.
- The section on 'Continuing the story …' at the end of the book will give some suggestions about practical outworking in your own context.
- You are welcome to contact me at suepickering83@gmail.com.

NB While the focus of this book is on becoming disciples who are able to witness using face-to-face interaction, there will be times when sharing our God-song using modern technology will broaden access to a story of God's loving presence in human life. The growing use of technology and social media, especially among young people also means that we need to be in touch with

3 *A New Zealand Prayer Book*, http://anglicanprayerbook.nz/925.html.

ways of connecting that work for tech-savvy youth and others. As you work your way through this book, keep in mind how modern media might promote the gospel in your context. A website, podcasts, live streaming of special events, making music together and uploading it online, sharing Facebook posts or tweets relevant to different cultural groups in your neighbourhood, are all ways of using social media to show that followers of Jesus are deeply interested in the life of the community *beyond* the four walls of the church.

⌘

Now it's time to get started with the first set of reflection questions – may the journey through this book be a blessing to you and those to whom you sing your God-song.

Find somewhere you won't be interrupted. Switch off your mobile phone and put it aside for now. Have available some plain paper and coloured pencils/felt-tips for drawing, for example, a time line or symbolic representation of your spiritual journey. Ask the Holy Spirit to guide you; settle into silence and consider your God-song.

How did your God-song begin? What was your earliest awareness of God or Jesus?
How has love entered your life? Where was God?
When have you sensed an invitation/s to serve God/follow the Way of Jesus? What happened?

Now let yourself reflect on times when your life was full of lament or pain.
Where was God? How did such experiences affect the way you saw God then/see God now?

- As I've discovered personally, and in my experience of offering spiritual direction, it's not uncommon to find that the strength of our God-song varies over time, especially if we are heavily involved in ministry:
  - It may be silenced by the pressure of pastoral work when we are too busy to notice what God is doing around us, our energy is depleted and we become 'flat' and 'mechanical' in our interactions.
  - We may struggle to lift our voice above worry, discouragement or vexed intra-church dynamics.
  - Our song may sound hollow to our ears, as unexamined faith questions compromise our commitment.

Spend a few minutes reflecting on the current strength or weakness of your God-song.

If you are in 'good voice', give thanks to God; if not, speak, write or whisper to God about your situation, what has brought you to this point and what you long for.

The 'back-story'

'The Lord is here', a priest says at the start of the Great Thanksgiving,[1] and with the ritual, prayerfulness and sense of mystery, it's easy to grasp why we might feel nearer to God in church. Nor is it hard to understand why mission might be seen as 'taking God' out into a world unaware of its Creator.

Remnants of this 'God-in-a-backpack' attitude still linger in Christian consciousness, but if we stop to think about it, a god acting only within the 'church' or through its appointed ministers is a very limited god indeed. As Christians, we are called to worship a generous God, to follow Jesus: God with us by his Spirit, the Cosmic Christ, 'in whom all things hold together'.[2]

It follows that we should be able to notice signs of God's influence, presence and provision *beyond* the church in our diverse contexts and communities. As the late Dr David Hay[3] prophetically observed at a turn of the millennium conference for mission studies: 'one might see the mission of the Church as to be alert to – and be in tune with – the ways in which God is *already* in touch with everybody, *inside or outside the Church*.'[4]

---

1 *A New Zealand Prayer Book*, Collins, London, 1989, p. 420.

2 Colossians 1.17b.

3 Former director of the Religious Experience Research Unit in Oxford, founded by the zoologist Sir Alister Hardy in 1969 to test the hypothesis that religious experience was 'hard-wired' into human life; the Unit is now based at the University of Wales at Lampeter.

4 David Hay, 'The Spirituality of the Unchurched', conference paper, British and Irish Mission Association, 2000, based on research undertaken by D. Hay and K. Hunt, *Understanding the Spirituality of People Who don't go to Church*, Centre for the Study of Human Relations, University of Nottingham, 2000; emphasis mine.

If we believe our God *is already* walking ahead of us, working with or without us, sometimes in spite of us, being a witness can take on a whole new dynamic. Instead of lamenting the absence of God in our communities, we could go about our daily routines alert for signs of God's love, creativity and suffering in the people we encounter; we could have the privilege of discovering what matters to God in our neighbourhoods. Gradually the artificial division between sacred and secular would diminish.

I believe that, for a season, our continuously creative God is pushing us out of our drying-up ecclesiastical habitat into a kaleidoscope of communities, challenging us to be more effective partners in building God's kingdom of justice and peace, caring for each other and for our world. Ripples of this challenge have been spreading for years. You'll be aware of some from your own reading or experience; here are some of mine:

- In 2011 the writer and pastor Alan Roxburgh, though an established voice in mission and evangelism circles,[5] recognized the church-centred mindset of many of the books written about emerging forms of church and mission, and, with admirable humility, included some of his own. In doing so, he affirmed Lesslie Newbigin,[6] whose writing continually pointed to the interplay among culture, the gospel and the church. Roxburgh described Newbigin as being 'in a constant dialogue with the culture, in which he lived, and the gospel, which he loved … [not using] this culture to get somewhere else – he indwells it and through that indwelling reads again the biblical narratives to ask how the gospel could reengage his culture in his time.'[7]

- In the same year, a Church or England briefing document about Mission Action Plans stated: 'Much of the impetus for

---

5 See more about Alan Roxburgh's work and writing at http://themissionalnetwork.com/category/who/our-story.

6 Lesslie Newbigin was a missionary in India for decades. On his return to the UK in 1974, he found the culture shockingly changed – no longer did the Christian narrative hold a place, however tenuous, in the lives of the majority. His writing continues to challenge and inspire. See 'Further reading' for details of his works.

7 Alan J. Roxburgh, *Missional: Joining God in the Neighborhood*, Baker Books, Grand Rapids, MI, 2011, p. 42.

imaginative mission in recent years has been generated by the close encounter between a church and its social context. Mission has come to be seen, less as something defined by the church and offered to the world, and more as a dialogue between cultures and the church, conducted through careful interpretation and translation between distinctive "languages": the language of Christian theology and the language of local culture ... As the Fresh Expressions movement has helped us to understand ... [m]uch of the most effective mission activity of recent decades has been carefully and prayerfully responsive to local cultures, with the result that the church's mission is multifaceted and deeply contextualised.'[8]

- In his 2015 inaugural Lambeth Lecture. Archbishop Justin Welby spoke of a Church 'in which every Christian shares "the revolutionary love" of Jesus Christ'.[9] He commented that a 'seismic shift' is needed for this to happen – a powerful metaphor for a radical reshaping of how we might form disciples and empower witnesses. Unless Christians share naturally and fittingly their stories of grace and hope in Christ with those they meet in daily life, there will be no renewal.

- In 2016 the Anglican Consultative Council's report *Intentional Discipleship and Disciple-Making: An Anglican Guide for Christian Life and Formation*[10] was released. An exploration of the history and current practice of mission around the Anglican communion, this work rightly acknowledged those who 'are witnessing to Christ's reconciling love all over the world, and in all sorts of ways, as a sign of their discipleship'. But, the writers say, 'much more could be done if there was an *intentional* focus on nurturing and equipping both new and

8 Dr Philip Giddings, *Mission Action Planning in the Church of England: Briefing Note from the Mission and Public Affairs Council*, June 2011, paragraphs 6 and 7, p. 2, www.churchofengland.org/media/1281665/gs%201835b.pdf.

9 http://episcopaldigitalnetwork.com/ens/2015/03/12/welby-seismic-shift-required-to-equip-all-anglicans-as-evangelists/#.VQi4hPADacc.email.

10 John Kafwanka and Mark Oxbrow (eds), *Intentional Discipleship and Disciple-making: An Anglican Guide for Christian Life and Formation*, Anglican Consultative Council, London, 2016.

> existing members, to deepen their lifelong discipleship and Christian witness'.[11] They further comment that few Christians have been 'discipled to be missional people in the context of their everyday lives' and 'too few churches are structured in such a way that will enable a community of intentional disciples to be formed.'[12]

The 'seismic shift' to which Archbishop Welby referred is gathering momentum. Such a shift would require a change of culture so that churches foster *both* optimistic, neighbourhood-focused mission *and* the spiritual growth and deep joy of the gathered church, however and wherever it meets. This will not be easy. After all, seismic shifts can cause upheaval, fear and tsunami – and we will need a tsunami of grace in the years to come as we grapple with this call to be more purposeful about discipleship and witness.

But seismic shifts can also create opportunities for the new to flourish and for the strengthening and refreshment of the old so it is 'fit for purpose' in the twenty-first century and beyond. It is time for the institutional church to support lay people *in their vocation as God's witnesses in the world*, by intentionally weaving together the inward journey of formation as disciples and the outward journey of partnering God in God's world as witnesses to the transformative power of God's Spirit.

Statistics and media reports in the West might have us believe that the Christian faith is waning and the Church is in terminal decline, but despite this perception and the historical lack of formation in mission and witness in much ministry training and lay formation,[13] there *are* innovative community-based ministries flying below the radar. *Unrecognized* by media and *unheard of* by most Christians, people motivated by love for Jesus and empowered by his Spirit *are* making a difference in their communities, through a vast range of projects and new ways of being church; although they may seem like little ripples in a vast sea of indifference, ripples spread, and merge and grow.

---

11 Kafwanka, *Intentional Discipleship*, p. xii; emphasis mine.

12 Kafwanka and Oxbrow, *Intentional Discipleship*, p. 114.

13 Richard Randerson, *Engagement 21: A Wake-up call to the 21st Century Church in Mission*, Matai House, Wellington, NZ, 2010, pp. 10–12.

One day, we pray, 'the earth *will* be filled with the glory of God as the waters cover the sea'.

One day, *wherever* we find ourselves, *whatever* we are doing, and *whoever* we are with, may we come to know, with confidence and deep joy, that 'The Lord is here!'

PART I

Listening: becoming disciples

The first duty of love is to listen.
Paul Tillich

The story of how we become disciples

One of my favourite family photos shows my husband with the lawnmower and our son, then aged about four, standing happily beside him with his own little plastic mower. I remember how he used to follow his dad everywhere, trying to copy whatever he was doing. His first impulses to learn new skills naturally stemmed from this father–son relationship.

The word 'discipleship' takes its origin from the Latin *discere*, 'to learn'. Christian discipleship is clearly about learning to follow Jesus, and letting his Spirit show us how to make his way known in the world. At its best, discipleship happens in the context of growing our relationship with God – the Blessed Trinity. However, the Western cultural preference for reason and the acquisition of knowledge – learning *about* God – has exerted a strong influence on the Church for centuries. As a consequence, an understandable emphasis on studying Scripture and learning about the customs and doctrines of the tradition developed, often at the expense of developing a relationship *with* God.

To be effective disciples of Jesus, we need *both* understanding *and* relationship.

The earliest disciples learned directly from the Master, later disciples from those who had known him personally, and later still from those in whom his Spirit was alive and instructive. Their connection with Jesus was vibrant and real: understanding and relationship were closely bound. Today, unless we are intentionally discipled in such a way that our connection with Jesus by his Spirit is strengthened, that vital personal link with the 'pioneer and perfecter of our faith' (Hebrews 12.2) can be obscured by an overload of information; it can be like trying to follow someone whom we've heard a lot about but never met.

- How have you been discipled up to this point?
You may like to draw a timeline with significant people/events/decisions and so on to help you name the influences that, over time, drew you closer to God.
It might also be helpful to acknowledge anything that has hindered your following Jesus.

- What discipleship programmes/initiatives have you been part of as a participant, as a leader?
What has been the 'fruit' of that participation?
What questions have been raised for you?

Each of us has a unique story of how we've been discipled. For me there was little overt Christian practice in my family until we came to New Zealand. Then we joined an Anglican church and I did the conventional things – attended Bible class, was prepared for confirmation, taught Sunday school, had a brief insight into the reality of Jesus after a Billy Graham campaign, but then drifted spiritually in my 20s. I'd been exposed to the Christian story in a fairly typical way but I wasn't a disciple and never witnessed.

> Everything changed in my 30s. I became very depressed, even suicidal. Desperate, I poured out my story to a woman[1] who listened with deep compassion and, at the end of our conversation, simply said, 'What you need is Jesus Christ.' Something deep within me knew she was right. A Life in the Spirit seminar was due to start soon at her local church so I went along. After the second session I felt dubious about the whole thing, but something impelled me to go to the small wooden church alone one mid-week morning. I knelt there in the silence and then offered to God my despair and the tiny part of myself that genuinely wanted to trust. Nothing happened. I waited for a while, then went out and drove home. And that is when I started to sing in a language I'd never learned; that was my Thomas moment, the start of 'My Lord and my God' reality.

1 I found out later that the woman to whom I had been drawn had prayed before we met, and was prompted by the Holy Spirit to speak those closing words to me.

God gave me what I needed – the gift of tongues to strengthen my spirit and bypass my busy, anxious, rational mind, and the embrace of a small group of older Christian women who held me literally and prayerfully, gently discipling me until I was on the Way and able to respond when God opened new doors over the next 30 years.

The first such door opened in the context of an 18-month ecumenical lay assistant hospital chaplaincy course. Meeting fortnightly, we five participants and the hospital chaplain *began* by sharing our stories at depth, a process that built trust, respect and enduring friendship. We were provided with succinct and relevant information, watched others to see how pastoral visiting might be done, tried it for ourselves, wrote verbatim, reflected theologically and talked over issues afterwards. Within that safe and confidential setting, I began to learn more about myself, more about God, about other people's suffering and courage, and about healing vis-à-vis cure.

Other opportunities included a four-year Education for Ministry programme;[2] spiritual direction formation and leadership; regular times of retreat, reflection and deepening contemplative prayer; engagement with Scripture, particularly the Gospels, which drew me into Jesus' humanity and divinity; the chance to spend time in Israel; the privilege and responsibilities of priesthood; the unexpected call to aged care chaplaincy – and always, the invitation to follow Jesus and let God's love flow through me as I connected more deeply with the people whom God brought across my path.

What elements in your discipleship worked for you (e.g. small groups, making music, sharing food)?

One of the greatest illnesses in our developed world is *disconnection*. People are increasingly removed from their families and neighbours by distance or disaffection; cut off from the natural world by intensification of urban living; too busy to stop and catch up with themselves; and out of touch with God. Effective

2 A theological education distance programme based on small groups and practice. See more at http://efm.sewanee.edu.

discipleship *connects* us with our God and with our own light and shadow; it strengthens our *connection* with creation and the people around us, including those on the margins. In the process of learning to follow Jesus, we can be transformed from isolated, egocentric individuals to God-centred members of creative communities who fulfil our potential as daughters and sons of a loving, faithful God. We can make a difference in our world as we sing of the God who is here.

Listening to God, Jesus and Holy Spirit

> 'This is my Son, my Beloved: listen to him!'
> *Luke 9.35*

Echoing through the prophets and the psalms is the divine plea for the nation of Israel to *listen to God.* In spite of people's dogged rebellion and corporate deafness, God continued to offer covenant relationship and fullness of life, and that offer remains open for us. In the story of the transfiguration (Luke 9.28–36), those closest to Jesus saw his glorious essence revealed, heard the love of God for his dear Son proclaimed and, in no uncertain terms, *were told to listen to Jesus.*

God's message hasn't changed – God wanted the disciples to listen then and wants us to listen now – as a church, as small groups, and as individuals. Jesus is always worth listening to, not least because he's consistently countercultural and focused on connecting people with God. Take for example his turning the conventional 'master–slave' relationship of his day on its head with these words:

> I do not call you servants any longer, because the servant does not know what the master is doing; but I have called you *friends*, because I have made known to you everything that I have heard from my Father.
> *John 15.15*

We are offered friendship with God in Jesus, an intimate, robust bond of mutual trust as love seeks to overcome the resistance embedded in our nature. Yet if Jesus asked each one of us, 'Who do you say that I am?'[1] how many would respond, 'You're my friend'? How many of us would know the truth of that relationship deep within our soul and let it shape our willingness to listen to God, to be loved by God, and to witness to God's love in the world?

Take some time out to reflect on how you respond to Jesus' offer of friendship.

⌘

Through the action of the Holy Spirit *we learn to listen to God* in many ways, but for the purpose of forming disciples, we're going to focus on three: creation, Scripture and silence.

Creation – the first book

Like the psalmist, we may be accustomed to seeing in the natural world a reflection of God's beauty, grandeur or strength: 'The heavens are telling the glory of God; and the firmament proclaims his handiwork' (Psalm 19.1). We marvel at the complexity of the commonplace – beehives, whale communication, nest-building; in the midst of rush and routine we may have our favourite places of peace and comfort – park, stream, tree house or allotment, which help us sense that something 'other' we name as God. Poets such as Hopkins and Oliver[2] help us see something of creation's hidden holiness; Elizabeth Barrett Browning bemoaned humanity's inability to see the divine woven through the natural world:

> Earth's crammed with heaven,
> And every common bush afire with God;
> But only he who sees, takes off his shoes,
> The rest sit round it and pluck blackberries.[3]

---

1 The 'synoptic' Gospels Mark, Matthew and Luke, are so called because they contain similar stories and sometimes similar words. In this case the same words are used in Matthew 16.15, Mark 8.29 and Luke 9.20.

2 Gerald Manley Hopkins and Mary Oliver – see 'Further reading'.

3 Elizabeth Barrett Browning, 'Aurora Light', found at www.bartleby.com/236/86.html.

Not only *is* the creation brimming with the life and love of God, it can be a means through which God reaches out to us when we stop to 'take a long loving look at the real'.[4]

> On a recent retreat 'Tom' was struggling with a difficult ministry transition. He was anxious and could not see a positive way forward. As he walked the grounds of the retreat house, he was drawn to what seemed a dry rose bush, thinking that it aptly reflected his own state of mind and spirit. But when he stopped, bent down and looked more closely, he saw a single bud just beginning to swell. His eyes moistened. He said later that it was as if God were reminding him that, even though he felt dry and lost, new life was taking shape quietly and would bud and blossom in time.

Through the simplest of interactions with the creation around us, in gardens or parks, through the sky, sea or our pets, God can teach us truths about ourselves and about God's nature, if we stop to listen:

> Pickles, my once soppy little tabby, has grown into a strong-willed young cat intent on exploring. She no longer wants to sit on my lap and look at me with love, purring and kneading her way into kitten dreamland. One day, as I reflected on how much I missed her affection, I realized that God misses me, misses all of us when we are determinedly independent and want to do everything *except* sit still with God, let ourselves be loved, and love God as best we can in return.

🕯 What's your experience of stopping long enough to let some aspect of the creation become for you a messenger of God?

⌘

4 Walter Burghardt's definition of 'contemplation', taken from www.facebook.com/notes/ignatian-spirituality/contemplation-a-long-loving-look-at-the-real/96538280841.

The natural world can be the primary 'voice' of the sacred for countless people disaffected by religious structures. For example, we might hear people speak of feeling peace or 'connectedness' when outdoors walking on the beach or looking at the night sky. This spiritual bond is a catalyst for action: people's growing compassion for the natural world, in the face of species decline, disappearance of habitat, the effects of global warming and natural disasters, has led to a proliferation of movements addressing the damage caused by humanity's poor stewardship of the earth and its resources.

'Care of creation' can be common ground when we are moving among people outside the church environment, but it can also – justifiably – be a point of challenge, because of our collective Christian deafness to the 'whole earth groaning as in labour' (Romans 8.22). Yes, Christians are well represented in the running and establishment of aid agencies and disaster relief, but at the World Conservation Congress held in Hawaii in September 2016, among the 9,000 delegates there was *only one* international Christian conservation organization: A Rocha, founded by two Christian families in the 1980s and now a global network of conservation projects in more than 20 countries.[5]

If we stopped long enough to listen as a local church, what might God want to say to us about our neglect of creation in our own neighbourhood?
How are you and/or your congregation involved in any project to conserve your local environment?

Scripture: the second book

As we read the Bible we build up an awareness of God's nature and dealings with humanity, and the ways and work of Jesus and the Holy Spirit; we become familiar with the stories of countless ordinary people whose lives and struggles remain surprisingly relevant in our contemporary context because human nature hasn't

5 A Rocha, founded by Peter and Miranda Harris and Leslie and Wendy Batty, has been engaging communities in conservation since the early 1980s: http://blog.arocha.org/en/why-conservation-is-a-gospel-issue.

changed; and we 'bank' a range of Scripture verses, which the Holy Spirit can bring to mind when we need them.[6] We may have spent years studying Scripture and noting passages' relevance to our lives or inspiration for service, but it's possible that we have never been introduced to the practice of *praying* with Scripture in a way that opens deeper insights and encourages us to rest in God.

What is your experience of praying with Scripture in contrast to studying it or using it to preach/teach?

Imaginatively praying with Scripture (a method developed by St Ignatius) encourages us to enter a Gospel passage using our senses – seeing, smelling, tasting, touching and hearing the story set in the time of Jesus. Or we can bring the location into the present day and imagine the story unfolding somewhere familiar to us: the local café, the high street, park or factory. Either way we can put our imagination into the safe hands of God and witness a miracle, be one of the disciples or a person healed, and get closer to what it might have been like for Jesus. Some people can listen to God through Scripture better this way than through a rational approach.

Another way of praying with Scripture suits a wider range of people and brings us closer to the third 'book' of God: silence. In the first millennium *lectio divina* (sacred reading of *small*[7] portions of Scripture) was how prayer was taught. This way of reading, reflecting, responding and resting in God was available to all who wanted to pray. Just as the Lord's Prayer was taught to all people without discrimination, so moving into contemplation was seen as a natural part of prayer for everyone, not just the preserve of a religious élite. But sadly, early in the second millennium, as reason and analysis began to dominate the primary routes to knowledge, including knowledge of God, the soul-nourishing 'resting in God' step fell away and, for ordinary folk, access to the deep well of grace in contemplation withered away. Thankfully this way of

6 See for example Ephesians 6.17: 'Take the helmet of salvation, and the sword of the Spirit, which is the word of God.'

7 Where access to Scripture was limited, the small portion would be read aloud over and over again – so the word could indeed 'dwell in us richly' (Colossians 3.16).

praying with Scripture is being reclaimed, helping us make our home in the word of God, and enabling us to move into contemplative prayer in a natural way:

- ***Lectio***: super-slow reading of a *small*[8] portion of Scripture aloud (two or three times) to allow something to take our attention.
- ***Meditatio***: thinking about what we've noticed or not noticed, how it connects with our life, what it might have to say about the culture of which we are a part, generally mulling it over.
- ***Oratio***: communicating with God about what we've discovered or what we are feeling – talk, write, sing, dance or in some other suitable way tell God what's been prompted by the passage.
- ***Contemplatio***: stopping intellectual activity – simply allowing ourselves to abide in God, to rest like a satisfied baby on its mother's knee, quietly allowing God to be with us in love (Psalm 131).

You may already be familiar with some form of the first three parts of this process, but it is the final movement, *contemplatio*, the very part that fell from use centuries ago, that carries us gently into listening prayer. The part that it is tempting to ignore is also the part that provides us with deeper life.

Silence: the third book

Just as we can't fully communicate with someone who is deaf unless we've learned sign language, our communication with God will remain limited until we become proficient in a less familiar but profound God-language. Elijah stumbled across it, running from Jezebel:

> He [the LORD] said, 'Go out and stand on the mountain before the LORD, for the LORD is about to pass by.' Now there was a

8 A few verses from the Gospels draw us closer to Jesus; a small portion of a psalm models honest communication with God!

> great wind, so strong that it was splitting mountains and breaking rocks in pieces before the LORD, but the LORD was not in the wind; and after the wind an earthquake, but the LORD was not in the earthquake; and after the earthquake a fire, but the LORD was not in the fire; and after the fire a sound of sheer silence.
> *1 Kings 19.11–12*

Thomas Keating, teacher of 'centring prayer', wrote of it when he said:

> 'God's first language is silence. Everything else is a poor translation.'[9]

🕯 What's your response to the idea of God's 'first' language being silence?

Scripture reminds us to be still (Psalm 46.10), to wait upon God in silence, (Psalm 62.1, 5), so that we may be receptive, even in the midst of the day's comings and goings.

> Eleanor, in her 90s, told the story of her visit to the foothills of the Himalayas decades ago. Alone on the remote hotel's balcony, she stood, and looked, and waited. As Eleanor took in that profound silence, she experienced the peace of God – not with words or high emotion but with a rich inner knowing, a sense of being loved and held. She had found the truth of God's silence – that it was not the cold silence of apathy or disappointment but the intimate, inhabited silence of loving relationship. Eleanor was blessed by this knowing for the rest of her life, and it comforted her in her dying.

Regularly abiding in the silence of God[10] frees our mind from the onslaught of stimulation around us and sustains the listening space in our spirit, so we are more able to notice the bidding of the *Holy* Spirit.

---

9 Thomas Keating, *Invitation to Love: The Way of Christian Contemplation*, Continuum, New York, 1995, p. 90.

10 Or what we might call 'adopting a contemplative stance'.

As we intentionally engage in listening[11] prayer, whether we 'feel anything', receive insights, fight sleep or are so besieged by distractions that we have to bring ourselves repeatedly back to our anchor in Christ, *does not matter*. What we are doing is 'consenting to the work of God within us',[12] giving God space and time to do some divine loosening of our ego's rigid boundaries and defences, opening us up to be a conduit of God's love, freeing us to serve God with increasing energy and focus. That is why listening to God both strengthens discipleship and informs witness.

Our Western culture's avoidance of listening and silence[13] is echoed in much contemporary public worship. The fast-paced liturgy is commonly devoid of space in which to notice the whisper of grace. Even when it comes to confession, there is rarely time to gather or express our thoughts, before the absolution.

This absence of reflective space is found as well in our meetings, and even in study groups, as if we are all infected with the 'busyness' virus and think silence is non-productive. Nothing is further from the truth: from the silence of contemplative prayer, clarity of discernment and inspiration for action will emerge.

Many people in the general population are unaware of the long Christian tradition of contemplative spirituality, nor have many who were brought up as Christians ever encountered 'listening prayer'. Among some conservative Christians, the word 'meditation' provokes anxiety or derision because of its association with eastern spiritualities, yet in the Hebrew Bible 'meditation' means reflecting on the law,[14] and in recent decades has come to refer to a listening prayer practice promoted by the World Community for Christian Meditation. Alongside WCCM, Contemplative Outreach has developed a slightly different process to come to stillness and deepen contemplative prayer.[15] This process is called

---

11 I am using 'listening prayer' and 'contemplative prayer' interchangeably for ease of discussion.

12 As Thomas Keating would say in his introduction to centring prayer. Visit www.contemplativeoutreach.org.

13 Alfred Brendel's quote, 'The word "listen" contains the same letters as the word "silent"', first alerted me to this.

14 E.g. in Psalm 1.2, 'but their delight is in the law of the LORD, and on his law they *meditate* day and night.'

15 For the websites of WCCM and Contemplative Outreach, see 'Further reading'.

'centring prayer' (see 'Further reading') and enables practitioners to maintain silence by returning to an 'anchor' word whenever distractions threaten to derail our intention to be still before God.

In contemporary Christian circles, there appears to be a widening interest in reconnecting with ancient spiritual practices, including listening/contemplative prayer, *lectio divina*, monastic rhythms, discerning a rule of life. A number of new monastic ventures have been popping up around the world in the last 15 to 20 years These communities may be dispersed or gathered, permanent or short-term, formal or informal, but have at their heart a desire to serve God's mission by offering regular prayer for the world alongside personal and group transformation, within a community of faith.[16]

⌘

Going Deeper: Listening to God

- Imagine yourself witnessing the transfiguration, hearing God's voice saying to you, 'Listen to Jesus!'
  How do you respond?
- What is your experience of silence? Bring any painful memories or current resistance to God.
- How might attending to creation and Scripture, and being still before God, be woven into the fabric of your day or your congregational practice?
- Use a few verses from one of you daily Bible readings for *lectio divina*.
- What is your initial response to the word 'meditation'?
  Talk to God about any anxiety, reluctance or joyful anticipation.

16 For the websites of the Community of St Anselm (Lambeth Palace) and Contemplative Fire (global), see 'Further reading'.

Listening to others

I remember so clearly being in labour 33 years ago and the words of the midwife, 'Do you want to have this baby or not?' I felt like yelling at her, but being an introvert I just gritted my teeth and pushed. She was a friend and she listened to what I wasn't saying, knowing from her considerable experience that I needed something to fire me into that final effort. And she was right – soon I was looking into the big brown eyes of our little boy.

In her book, *Holy Listening*, Revd Dr Margaret Guenther[1] uses the metaphor of the *midwife* to describe the privileged role of the pastoral listener/spiritual director in helping another person put words around her experience of God. The midwife's role is not to do the work for the labouring mother but to assess progress, work out what is going to be most helpful, and celebrate or lament together when the struggle is over.

Similarly, as pastoral listeners we do not try to shape the experience of those we listen to according to our understanding or tradition. Instead we listen with them for signs of grace, for what God – recognized or unrecognized – might be doing in their life. We offer them our loving focus, actively listening to what is and is not being said, alert to significant changes in any key relationships, and helping them pay attention to where Love is present in their lives.

- Think back over your week: make a list of the qualities that make listening 'holy'.

⌘

1 Margaret Guenther, *Holy Listening: The Art of Spiritual Direction*, Cowley Publications, Cambridge, MA, 1992.

Listening to others

If we are honest, we often struggle to listen well. Our attention span is affected by ever-shortening sound bytes in the media; we are distracted by various beeps from devices near at hand; voices are overwhelmed by music, music spoilt by voice-overs; the speed of speech and unfamiliar accents hamper comprehension; and, to be honest, sometimes we have to work hard to overcome initial dislike, or even anxiety, before we can commit ourselves to paying attention rather than running away.

However, if we can stop and give someone our *full* attention even for a few minutes, if we are not driven by the compulsion to fix things or 'save souls', then our kindness and the loving presence of God flowing through us means that a person can feel 'seen and heard' and be drawn, gently, closer to God.

But what do we do with what we hear? People rightly expect us to be models of discretion; any breach of confidence can damage both relationships and reputation. It is too easy to give inappropriate detail in prayer chains or staff meetings; our spouse may be curious about pastoral visits; even in supervision, identifying detail must be kept out of the conversation. There is one exception: maintaining confidentiality takes second place when the person with whom we are talking is at imminent risk of self-harm or hurting others. In that case we act to ensure their safety (and that of others and ourselves) by arranging prompt medical referral or crisis-team intervention.

Which of the situations below could be described as 'holy listening'?

- A teacher waits while a stuttering child finds her next word.
- A man listens for half an hour as his partner pours out the joy of his first day at his new job.
- An old woman sits listening to the gaps between the breaths of her dying husband.
- A priest comes to anoint a woman before surgery and sits with her as she speaks of her fear.
- A city dweller hears a blackbird call above the traffic din and stops for a few minutes.
- An office worker offers tissues as her colleague speaks of her broken relationship.

- o A child lies on the floor beside his kitten as it purrs.
- o An urban search-and-rescue team calls for silence amid post-earthquake rubble.

Notice your thoughts and feelings – such as questions raised or reactions that are uncomfortable.
Then revisit your earlier response to what you would regard as 'holy listening'.

The common factor in the situations above is the quality of the presence of the listener. There is no superficial, distracted, haphazard attention but deep relational engagement *with the other*. Overt God-language may or may not be present, but the loving Spirit of God is.

Holy listening happens when we can be a non-anxious presence, able to listen fearlessly:

- o to the other person with the ears, heart and mind of Jesus
- o to ourselves well enough to notice our responses and manage them so we don't hinder the other person's story or sharing
- o to the Holy Spirit within us, alert for a word in season, a question to open up the conversation or an expression of compassion or encouragement.

Listening well to others takes on new significance in conversations with those struggling with church attendance, or those we meet who have left but continue to profess a belief in God – and there are many of these 'churchless Christians'. In 2001, when the term appeared in the *World Christian Encyclopaedia*,[2] it was estimated that there were 112 million worldwide, a number predicted to double by 2025.

In 2002 the New Zealand pastor and sociologist Alan Jamieson[3] wrote the first of several books researching church leavers. He discovered that many were leaving not because they had lost their

2 David Barret, George Thomas Kurian and Todd M. Johnson, *World Christian Encyclopaedia*, 2nd edn, Oxford University Press, Oxford, 2001.

3 Alan Jamieson, *A Churchless Faith: Faith Journeys beyond the Churches*, SPCK, London, 2002; *Called Again: In and beyond the Deserts of Faith*, Philip Garside, Wellington, NZ, 2004; and *Five Years On: Continuing Faith Journeys of Those who Left the Church*, Portland Research Trust, Wellington, NZ, 2006.

faith but because they could no longer remain within religious institutions where they were not heard; where there was no space for questions and deepening of faith, and more concern with 'in-house' matters than seriously equipping people to join Jesus in a hurting world. Small groups of like-minded 'exiles' from the institutional church can often be a blessing to their communities but do so without the support and accountability which, at its best, the institutional church can provide.

A 2012–13 study of 'de-churched' people in Scotland conducted by the mission development worker Dr Steve Aisthorpe[4] discovered that, together with the reasons Jamieson lists above, people left because they were concerned about congregations' unwillingness to change, leadership's inability to manage conflict, and above all because the call to be witnesses for Christ in the world was more talked about than practised.

Jamieson reminds us that, above all, people who are becoming disenchanted, have left or have never attended need to be listened to without judgement. We are to take people's stories at face value whether they include criticism, biblical misunderstanding or accounts of unanswered prayer, for this is their truth at that point. We do not need to defend God or engage in heated debate. Rather we 'turn the other cheek', accepting that the person's position 'is what it is' – and may change – particularly if we continue our conversation over a long period and include them in our prayers!

By adopting a non-defensive position we may enable someone to tell their story at a deeper level. We enter that hurting place gently; we listen to their anguish and absorb some of their pain, bringing their distress to Jesus in prayer with and for them. That is what builds relationship and strengthens connection.

'As we listen, we change', Jamieson wisely says. 'In such pastoral listening – non-judgemental, provisional, face-value, long-term, painful listening ... lies the hope of the church of the future.'[5]

⌘

4 Reported by Madeleine Davies, *Church Times*, 24 March 2016. See 'Further reading' for Aisthorpe's book based on this research.

5 Alan Jamieson, Jenny McIntosh and Adrienne Thompson, *Five Years On*, Portland Research Trust, Wellington, NZ, 2006, pp. 112–13.

Going Deeper: Listening to Others

- Over a few days, make some notes about your listening behaviour, particularly in relation to the quality/quantity of your interactions with others. If you are an extrovert, it may be that listening without interrupting is harder than you had imagined! Take this dilemma to prayer.

- How would you rate your listening skills?
  Do you listen 'in order to respond' or listen 'in order to learn'?
  If you haven't already undergone training in active listening, consider upskilling, for example through Samaritans, local community education courses or diocesan education programmes.

- 'You can learn to love anyone if you take long enough to hear their story.'
  How do you respond to this quote by a social worker?[6]

- What is your experience of listening to people who are struggling to stay in the church or those who have become 'churchless Christians'?
  What was it like for you to hear criticism of the church you love or the God you serve?

6 Jonny and Esther Grant (eds), *St Pauls Stories*, St Paul's Anglican Church, Auckland, NZ, p. 5.

Listening to ourselves: Disciplines and discernment

> 'Why do you see the speck in your neighbour's eye, but do not notice the log in your own eye? [4]Or how can you say to your neighbour, "Let me take the speck out of your eye", while the log is in your own eye? [5]You hypocrite, first take the log out of your own eye, and then you will see clearly to take the speck out of your neighbour's eye.'
>
> *Matthew 7.3–5*

In our early years we develop strategies for dealing with the challenges we encounter, and often that means unconsciously hiding who we really are by pretending we like something when we don't, hiding our feelings and adopting a mask or persona, showing our 'best' but 'false' self to the world – and to God – in order to gain approval or minimize pain.

Sooner or later, however, cracks will appear in this carefully constructed public image – we begin to make mistakes; we fail to live up to our own or others' expectations; we can no longer pretend to have it all together when anxiety, illness, or work problems make it patently clear that something must change.

Jesus' strong words signal the necessity of noticing what's going on in our emotional and thought life so we can look after ourselves and minimize the hurt we cause to others. Just as the prodigal son in Luke 15 'came to himself', so we are challenged to make conscious or 'bring to the surface' our hidden motivations, fears, wounds and prejudices so they can be faced, offered to God and redeemed. God longs to transform us, to bring us back to our original uniqueness, our 'true self' where God's image in us is clear and bright.

As the psychiatrist and spiritual director David Benner says:

> Every moment of every day of our life God wanders in our inner garden, seeking companionship ... The reason God can't find us is that we are hiding in the bushes of our false self. God's call to us is gentle and persistent: 'Where are you? Why are you hiding?'[1]

🕯 Allow yourself a few minutes to connect with this description of God's longing and human resistance. You may want to imagine yourself hiding from God (like Adam and Eve!), and see what happens when God comes looking for you in love.

⌘

It's tempting to let the busyness of our day wash through our synapses without stopping for reflection, hoping it's processed during our dream sleep. But unless we take time to listen to ourselves, to notice what themes are emerging and what emotions are being triggered, there can be no transformation; we won't be able to sing our God-songs freely, or risk removing the mask we've been taught – or chosen – to wear.

For a very few people – such as the apostle Paul[2] – transformation is sudden and shocking: one moment breathing wrath and threat upon Jesus' followers as he travelled towards Damascus; the next brought to utter vulnerability, Saul's public image shattered by the very One whom he persecuted. A period of dependency and tomb-like darkness gave Saul space for sustained reflection. And then came his own 'resurrection' day, when obedient, courageous Ananias brought God's healing, called Saul 'brother' and confirmed the reality of his meeting with Jesus on the Damascus road, a story Paul would tell and retell for the rest of his life.

Less familiar is the contemporary story of Sara Miles' powerful encounter with Jesus:

---

1 David Benner, *The Gift of Being Yourself*, Inter-Varsity Press, Downers Grove, IL, 2004, p. 81.

2 Acts 9.

> One early, cloudy morning when I was 46, I walked into a church, ate a piece of bread, took a sip of wine. A routine Sunday activity for tens of millions of Americans – except that up until that moment I'd led a thoroughly secular life, at best indifferent to religion, more often appalled by its fundamentalist crusades. This was my first communion. It changed everything.
>
> Eating Jesus, as I did that day to my great astonishment, led me against all my expectations to a faith I'd scorned and work I'd never imagined. The mysterious sacrament turned out to be not a symbolic wafer at all but actual food – indeed, the bread of life. In that shocking moment of communion, filled with a deep desire to reach for and become part of a body, I realized what I'd been doing with my life all along was what I was meant to do: feed people.[3]

Sara's sudden transformation was tailor-made for her and for the needs God sought to meet through her particular set of talents and personality. From the altar of her church Sara went on to feed thousands of those on the margins and to tackle some of the inequity that led to their impoverishment.

For most of us, however, transformation is more like the experience of the apostle Peter: his blustery self-confidence was *slowly* altered by his years with Jesus and his exposure to the 'otherness', the holiness of Jesus. Peter's way of seeing himself as brave and loyal to Jesus to the end was, like Paul's self-image, completely undone by his predicted, triple betrayal after Jesus' arrest. Propelled into abject self-loathing and grief, Peter was understandably cautious until the post-resurrection healing on the beach, when Jesus gave Peter the opportunity to restate his commitment to Christ for all to see. From then on, Peter's transformation shines through the book of Acts and continues to echo through the centuries, inspiring us to believe that the power of God to transform is greater than our selfishness and self-protective impulses.

Augustine wrote in his *Confessions*: 'Grant, Lord, that I may know myself that I may know thee.' Transformation happens

3 Sara Miles, *Take this Bread: A Radical Conversion*, Canterbury Press, Norwich, 2012.

as we become increasingly aware of who we are and welcome God's life in us in spite of our weakness and inner wounds. In the gradual process of sanctification, the Spirit moves us from self-centred to God-centred, develops the fruit of the Spirit within us[4] and shifts our focus from a narrow concern with what will make us safe and secure to the bigger picture: what can I do to contribute to God's world and make it a better place? Such grace-powered transformation enables us to bear the Christ-light to others and, ultimately, to experience theosis,[5] union with God in Christ through the Spirit.

There are many models of spiritual growth, from sixteenth-century Teresa of Avila's *Interior Castle*, with its journey through seven mansions to the innermost dwelling where the soul is united with God, to the contemporary classic, James Fowler's *Stages of Faith*, and Nicola Slee's *Women's Faith Development* (see 'Further reading'). For our purposes, however, I'm going to adopt Walter Brueggemann's pattern of orientation, disorientation and re-orientation[6] to explore briefly how our life of faith and image of God might unfold:

- ***Orientation***: initial exposure to the faith of our parents/caregivers/powerful others. Our way of seeing God is strongly influenced by those who are 'as God' to us. Through them we may glimpse God's unconditional love, be embraced by a warm community of faith and be taught to pray; or we may be subject to haphazard parenting with vague threats of some celestial policeman who watches everything we do – and doesn't like it – or us; or we may be exposed to abuse – emotional, physical, sexual or spiritual, which can corrupt our God-image and challenge our God-connection. The resulting distorted image of God as scathing perfectionist, punitive parent or unpredictable spoilsport can taint the rest of our

4 Galatians 5.22–23: 'love, joy, peace, patience, kindness, generosity, faithfulness, gentleness and self-control'.

5 According to Athanasius, *theosis* is 'becoming by grace what God is by nature' (*De Incarnatione*, I).

6 Walter Brueggemann, *Spirituality of the Psalms*, Fortress Press, Minneapolis, MN, 2002.

lives, unless we are encouraged to face it, re-examine it and discover for ourselves the God whom Jesus reveals.

- ***Disorientation***: often starting in early/mid adolescence but maybe much later, this uncomfortable period re-examines earlier understandings and experiences of God/Church in the light of emerging independence. This does not have to mean a loss of faith; rather it's about wrestling with doubts, inconsistencies and the state of the world around us. The period of disorientation may be precipitated by personal loss, intellectual challenge, a natural disaster, an act of terrorism or an ongoing conflict in which the suffering of innocents rightly threatens our notion of an 'all-powerful', 'good' God. This disorientation can propel us into a robust and necessary reassessment of who we think God is and how God works in the world. Sadly, however, many struggle with or leave institutional Christianity at this point, because, few churches cater well for people whose beliefs no longer fit the world they inhabit from Monday to Saturday.

> Why does the Church struggle in this area?
> Maybe we fear our own faith-faltering.
> Maybe we do not trust God to meet people in this liminal space.
> Maybe we've not done our own exploring and allowed God to guide us through our own uncertainty to a place of reorientation.

But the psalms give us hope – through them we see disorientation expressed through lament, anger, questioning and *crying out to God*, which keeps the connection between the psalmist and God alive, in spite of scepticism or deep emotional pain. If we can model and encourage such honest communication when people are struggling with their faith; if we can listen to their questions and honour the integrity of their searching, we will help them move towards the next step.[7]

---

7 During the period of 'disorientation', competent spiritual direction comes into its own.

- ***Re-orientation***: if we are well supported through this 'valley of the shadow', we may emerge with many of our original beliefs reworked and claimed as our own. We may, however, have changed some of the ways of thinking, praying or worshipping God; we may have come to an inner truce where the paradoxes and mystery of life are accepted, where we move from the dualistic 'and/or' approach to life, to the non-dual 'both/and' way of inclusiveness and creative solutions, a subtle, Christ-centred third way. We may entrust ourselves to a God who has chosen to keep us company in and through all things.

  This pattern is not a 'once and for all' process – it is repeated every time we encounter something that makes us question, affects us deeply or requires considered engagement with emerging social change, such as the 'right to die', the plight of refugees, the fair distribution of resources.

- How does the brief 'orientation/disorientation/reorientation' description of spiritual growth resonate with your experience – personally or as a pastoral minister?

⌘

Jesus invited his disciples and invites us to seek rest from the stress of 24/7 availability. For many of us this would include taking the opportunity to 'fast' from the use of digital devices, or choosing to take time off.

In Matthew 6.6 (*The Message*), Jesus says:

> Here's what I want you to do: Find a quiet, secluded place so you won't be tempted to role-play before God. Just be there as simply and honestly as you can manage. The focus will shift from you to God, and you will begin to sense his grace.

- Visualize Jesus inviting you to take some time to rest. Where would you choose to go? Picture what that place is like as clearly as you can or get a sense of how it feels when you're there. Then imagine Jesus meeting you in that place of rest, sitting quietly with you, with or without conversation. See what unfolds.

How do we begin to become gain self-knowledge? As always, with prayer for the grace we need to look within and the ability to recognize that God awaits us there. I've already mentioned the value of contemplative prayer, but there are other simple practices to help us 'listen to ourselves'. One of the most effective is the daily *examen*[8] – an end-of-day review developed by St Ignatius of Loyola – taking only a few minutes of reflection:

- Stillness – recalling God's presence here and now.
- Gratitude – expressing thankfulness.
- Reflection – looking back on your day.
- Sorrow – asking for forgiveness.
- Hopefulness – resolving to grow.[9]

As we bring our experience to consciousness and examine our behaviour in the light of the gospel, we begin to notice what has drawn us closer to God or pulled us further away The *examen* is not intended to be a vehicle for self-obsession, rather a way of gaining insight into our motivations, our desires and disappointments, and the extent to which we are following Jesus.

Other ways of listening to what is happening within are:

- Keeping a spiritual journal – for your eyes only – not a blog or something others will see. This may include notes and jottings, quotes, Bible commentary, pictures, lyrics, work with dreams, processing key family events, noticing God-moments, answered or unanswered prayers, sermon snippets – anything that relates to our inner life and spiritual formation.
- Noticing feelings. Because we've had more practice at noticing thoughts than feelings, it can be hard to recognize the way our bodies signal an emotional response, such as a tightened stomach, a dry mouth. But if we ignore our feelings we miss

8 See 'Further reading' for website information, or read *Sleeping with Bread* by Dennis Linn, Sheila Fabricant Linn and Matthew Linn, Paulist Press, New York, 1995, and available in a Kindle edition.

9 This particular pattern comes from the Jesuit website: www.loyolapress.com/our-catholic-faith/prayer/personal-prayer-life/different-ways-to-pray/prayerfully-reviewing-your-day-daily-examen.

vital information about our emotional well-being, spiritual needs, even our vocation Though many of us have been taught to suppress, mistrust, discount or disregard our feelings, Jesus freely expressed a full range of emotion.[10] We get closer to our own humanity and his, as we name our emotions and learn from them.

- Noticing our thought patterns. Pay attention to the tone and content of our self-talk – such as putting ourselves down/being kind and encouraging. Monitor the level of inner stress or anxiety present as different people or contexts come to mind. Get support promptly if thoughts turn towards self-harm.
- Reviewing our commitments. Busyness can signal spiritual laziness as we fill our diary and avoid spending time with ourselves and God. We deceive ourselves if we think our motives are totally altruistic, so it's always worth checking our motivation, asking, 'Why am I doing this? What am I getting out of this?'
- Meeting regularly with someone with whom we can confidentially share our faith journey. This person may be a spiritual director, a pastoral supervisor or a trusted friend who is strong enough to challenge us if need be. He/she is there to witness our desire to be accountable to God as we talk about our discoveries, seasons and struggles in the spiritual life.
- Being part of a small group engaging in theological reflection also provides a context for deeper self-awareness, as we shall see shortly.

Discernment – personal and group practices to aid decision-making

The process of discernment brings together listening to God *and* to ourselves and introduces other elements to help improve the accuracy of our listening, particularly when we are faced with major life choices or are trying to discern a way forward as a faith community. Psalm 119.105: 'Your word is a lamp for my feet and

---

10 Jesus' feelings: such as rage – John 12.15–16; frustration – Mark 9.19; grief – John 11.33–35; deep distress – Matthew 26.36–46.

a light to my path' encapsulates the discernment process: God often guides us one step at a time, as we:

- ask for the wisdom of the Spirit to guide the discernment process
- pay close attention to a triggering opportunity, challenge or unexpected invitation. We might use a list of pros and cons, or a business model, such as a SWOT analysis, which looks at strengths and weaknesses, threats and opportunities. We might use creativity to get 'inside' the possibilities offered
- notice the themes of Scripture readings around this time of discernment, and ask the Spirit to help us see how these might inform our emerging choice. God will not ask us to do anything that is contrary to God's nature as revealed in Scripture, and that nature is of course Love
- ask mature Christian friends to pray about the options we face and listen to their wisdom
- use common sense considering such things as our life stage, circumstances, family responsibilities, resources, health, abilities and weaknesses
- spend time in listening prayer, opening ourselves to the inner witness of the Holy Spirit – a sense of interior joy or anticipation, a 'stop' sign or a longing that draws us along a new path
- try the Quaker practice of the Clearness Committee[11] – a group discernment process in which the person presenting an issue for discernment sits with a group of others who prayerfully ask pertinent questions but *do not give advice or opinions*;
- stay alert for other ways God might use to communicate with us, such as dreams, synchronicity, a repetitive song or verse, an imaginative encounter during listening prayer.

No major decision can be based on a single discernment method – we begin with a provisional response and look for corroboration as we take each step. This can be a slow process and sometimes we have to trust that we are making the right decision *without*

11 See www.couragerenewal.org/clearnesscommittee for how this corporate approach to discernment works.

knowing how all the details will unfold, as happened for the Church Army couple David and Jen Pearce in 1981, when they accepted a role with World Vision in the Las Dhure refugee camp in Somalia.

Although David's job was titled 'Project Co-ordinator', when they flew into Singapore en route to their new posting, he'd been unable to find out exactly what was expected of him. Wrestling with God about their uncertainty, they attempted to contact a church nearby, but none of the churches they called answered the phone. Then David saw a World Vision office number and, in desperation, rang it. What followed has all the hallmarks of God's grace:

- a young man, who'd 'just popped into the office' to collect something, answered the phone
- he immediately arranged a meeting with a man who was in Singapore for *one night* on his way to Vietnam from London
- the man turned out to be the *Former Project Co-Ordinator* of the Las Dhure refugee camp – as David put it: 'He was the only man in the world who could brief me in a very real way on the work ... who to get to know, who to trust.'[12]

David and Jen had been prepared to act on what they sensed God was calling them to do, and had not hesitated to bring to God their anxiety about the lack of role clarity and contextual information.

God had answered them in a remarkable 'God-incidence' – an example of extraordinary provision and answer to prayer, which gave them an ongoing sense of confidence in God, and irrefutable evidence of God's provision, which sustained them through tough times.

⌘

12 David Pearce, *Kondoa 31: One Man's Journey Through Life*, self-published, 2015, pp. 49, 52.

Going Deeper: Listening to Ourselves

🕮 Pray with Jesus' question: 'What do you want me to do for you?' (Mark 10.51–52).

🕯 Look at the list on pages 27–8 of ways to increase awareness of self and God: daily review, journaling, noticing our thoughts and feelings and so on.
What reflective practice/s currently work/s well for you?
What might you change?
How might you ensure these practices are protected?

☺☹ Listen to your interactions with other people and notice such things as your tone of voice; whether you engage in gossiping or telling 'white lies' or agreeing with someone to avoid conflict; whether you give criticism or critique; whether you praise or patronize, build conflict or facilitate reconciliation; whether you habitually keep your opinions and ideas to yourself, contribute thoughtfully or dominate conversations. Talk to God and/or your spiritual companion about what you discover.

🕯 Consider the discernment process described above. Which 'methods' are familiar and which are new?

🕯 Look back to a major life decision: how did you discern the way you ultimately followed?
How much was God part of that process?
What might you do differently now if faced with another major decision?

'God-spotting': sharpening awareness of God in everyday life

We can't sing our God-song to others unless we are humming it to ourselves all day long.

We have nothing to hum unless we recognize God-moments as we move through our days and nights; unless we face each day trusting that, whatever happens, Jesus is indeed Emmanuel, 'God with us'.

In the early days of Christianity, Celtic Christians *intentionally* recalled God's Trinitarian presence, using prayers for every occasion, at every transition, in the routines of the day, in moments of danger and delight. They prayed with the whole of creation, conscious of the unity of all things in Christ, whose Spirit brings 'the whole world together as participants in the singing of one great hymn of praise'.[1] Perhaps it's because the Celts maintained their awareness of God with such devotion that their landscape still holds the memory of their prayer in 'thin places'[2] where God's presence is tangible.

Centuries later Brother Lawrence, a seventeenth-century Carmelite monk, gave us the precious phrase: 'practising the presence of God'. By this he meant *intentionally* bringing God to mind in the midst of the routines of life, just as the Celts did. Even as he 'turned this little omelette in the pan', he *consciously* did it in and for God. With practice, this intentional tuning in to God's song became embedded in his daily routine and, in love and gratitude, he was able, gently, to live out Paul's injunction:

1 Esther de Waal, *The Celtic Way of Prayer*, Hodder & Stoughton, London, 1996, p. 173.

2 See www.explorefaith.org/mystery/mysteryThinPlaces.html.

> And whatever you do, in word or deed, do everything in the name of the Lord Jesus, giving thanks to God the Father through him.
> *Colossians 3.17*

🕯 How aware are you of God or Jesus as you go through your day?
What helps or hinders this awareness?

As mentioned earlier, God does still meet people in unexpected and powerful ways appropriate to those people and the work to which God is calling them. Mostly, however, God self-reveals little by little so that we are not overwhelmed and so we can learn to listen to God's unfolding guidance and challenges in the stuff of ordinary life.

How *do* we become more aware of God's presence in our lives? We start by expanding our understanding of the *incarnation*. This term primarily refers to our awareness that Jesus was 'incarnate of the Holy Spirit and the Virgin Mary'[3] and left the exquisite unity of the Trinity for a life of separation, human struggle, occasional joy and pain beyond all comprehension. As Paul wrote in Philippians 2.7–8, Jesus:

> emptied himself, taking the form of a slave, being born in human likeness.
> And being found in human form, he humbled himself and became obedient to the point of death – even death on a cross.

Jesus – God incarnate – experienced suffering as a human being, and in his dying absorbed all evil before the blazing energy of his rising reorientated our entire world. This is a gutsy God who is not remote or disinterested, but is with us – no matter what. In the humanity and divinity of Jesus lie the core of our faith: God enters human experience, redeems our brokenness, enables ongoing God-connection with all people through the Holy Spirit, and reveals resurrection power available to us, *now*.

---

3 The Nicene Creed.

But there is another aspect to the incarnation that is often overlooked: humankind is made in the image of God. It follows that *everyone we meet bears the divine image*, irrespective of race, religion, sexual orientation or status. As Gerard Manley Hopkins wrote centuries ago:

> ... for Christ plays in ten thousand places,
> Lovely in limbs, and lovely in eyes not his
> To the Father through the features of men's faces.[4]

If we are willing, God, through the Spirit of Jesus, reaches out to us, guiding our discernment, encouraging and forgiving us. This holy helper brings words of Scripture directly to mind and offers practical tips, detailed instructions, timely dreams, nudges to action, economies of effort, moments of joy, reassuring common sense and inspiration for tasks ahead.

If we are willing, God, through the Holy Spirit, helps us to reach out to the people in our communities, inviting us to minister to each other with God's love and wisdom, bringing to life the words of St Teresa of Jesus (Ávila):[5] 'Christ has no body now but yours. No hands, no feet on earth but yours ...'[6]

If we are willing to receive from others, God, through the Holy Spirit can reach out to us through the people around us, if they are listening and respond.

Whether people are life-bearing or death-dealing, all are made with God-given abilities to reason, to be creative, to act justly, to be in loving relationship, to exercise free will; that image of God within each of us is beautified or diminished, as we choose to move closer to or further away from God.

4 'As Kingfishers Catch Fire', in Gerard Manley Hopkins, *Poems and Prose*, Penguin Classics, Harmondsworth, 1985; www.poetryfoundation.org/poems-and-poets/poems/detail/44389.

5 A Carmelite nun who was a strong and practical reformer of the faith in the difficult circumstances of sixteenth-century Spain.

6 For full quote visit: www.journeywithjesus.net/PoemsAndPrayers/Teresa_Of_Avila_Christ_Has_No_Body.shtml.

God-spotting: sharpening awareness of God in everyday life

After years working in the community in chaplaincy and church pastoral contexts, I've seen many people who, though raised as Christians, find it hard to believe they are 'good enough' to be agents of God's grace and so miss or resist opportunities to be a bearer of the 'Christ-light' in their neighbourhoods. Others struggle to accept that they actually matter to God, and so God's compassionate presence expressed through the loving acts of others goes unrecognized. We may sing songs like 'Brother, sister, let me serve you, let me be as Christ to you',[7] but fail to recognize that we really are 'as Christ to one another'.

Who has been the voice/hands/gaze of Christ for you in the last few weeks?
For whom have you been Christ's kindness, loving presence and warm smile?

⌘

Spot God in this story:

> A visitor to a bookshop noticed a little boy strapped securely to his dread-locked mother in a front-facing baby-pack. As the visitor browsed, he watched her ... Whenever she looked across at him, he would smile and so would she. Smiles were exchanged each time she emerged from behind a bookstand or rack of cards. He didn't tire of the 'game' – he kept on smiling and his eyes joined in. His gaze was unguarded and full of joy and when the visitor left that bookshop, there was a lightness in her step.

We might notice the love bond between mother and child and from there move on to:

- the gaze resting on the beloved – in this case the child's gaze resting on the visitor and her gaze on the child – reminding us of how God looks at the individual and us all
- the child – the joy and openness in his face affected the mood of the visitor as smiles grew
- the mutuality of acceptance and engagement

7 Richard Gillard, 'The Servant Song'.

- the *real* connection made in the few moments this encounter lasted.

'God-spotting' is doing what Jesus invited his listeners to do: '*Consider* the lilies ... the sower and the seed ... the fall of a sparrow ... the search for the lost sheep or coins, the return of prodigal son ...' Jesus was helping them *notice* God's faithfulness, care and kingdom in the midst of the ordinary things of their lives.[8] As we intentionally engage in God-spotting, we too can learn to make this connection and help others discover it for themselves.

How do we become adept at God-spotting?

We pray.

- We talk to God about our desire to be more aware of what God is doing each day.
- We practise listening prayer so our still centre is sustained and we are open to the Spirit.

We take the time to reflect when something catches our attention.

- We contemplate, slow down, and pause long enough to let God speak to us through the ordinary.

We take the incarnation seriously.

- We look for signs of movement towards Christ-likeness in our and others' lifestyles and priorities.
- We recognize that we are indeed the presence of Christ for others and we give thanks for the privilege of this reality (Matthew 25.40).
- When others help us, we recognize God in their voice, touch and care.

We become aware of the presence of Jesus wherever there is love *or suffering*.

- *Ubi caritas et amor, deus ibi est* is a familiar chant, which may be translated as: 'Where love and kindness[9] abound, God is there.'

---

8 Luke 12.27; Matthew 13.18–23; Luke 12.6; Luke 15.3–7, 8–10, 11–32.

9 *Caritas* may be translated as 'charity', which in common usage can mean detached giving or assistance, rather than personally costly engagement and support. Hence my use of the alternative 'kindness'. Sung by groups such as Taizé.

- *Ubi tribulatio et dolor, deus ibi est*, although not in common use, is complementary: 'Where suffering and grief abound, God is there.'

> Years ago, during the Second World War, Elie Wiesel[10] watched as a young boy was hanged in a concentration camp. Because he weighed so little, the young boy died a slow death, terrible for him and harrowing for all the witnesses. Wiesel heard someone mutter, 'Where's God in this?' There was silence for a moment, and then someone responded, 'He's there, hanging on the gibbet.'

If that same question were asked today, we might respond:

> 'He's there, sitting in the back of an ambulance in Aleppo, dusty from the rubble, trying to wipe the blood from his face.'[11]

In this child and countless others, we see the wounded Christ – God with us, being crucified over and over again, as human lust for power spirals out of control.

We are alert for hints of spiritual or religious[12] experience in people's lives.

Starting in the 1960s, the British scientist Sir Alister Hardy began testing the hypothesis that people had an inbuilt religious potential or awareness. He asked people a single question: 'Have you ever had a religious[13] experience or felt a presence or power, whether

10 https://writingforfoodinindy.wordpress.com/2013/02/06/where-is-god-reflecting-on-elie-wiesels-night.

11 www.aljazeera.com/news/2016/08/haunting-video-bewildered-syrian-boy-viral-160818080939606.html. The little boy's name is Omran Daqneesh. He was later released from hospital with light head injuries. God alone knows if he is still alive.

12 For our purposes, 'spiritual' relates to that which gives our lives deep meaning and purpose, the innermost part of ourselves (our 'essence'), that which connects us with ourselves, others, the world and the sacred; 'religious' relates to an organized set of beliefs and behaviours practised by a specific group of people that enables them to connect with their God and grow in service to others and to the world. For more on religious experience, see Sue Pickering, *Spiritual Direction: A Practical Introduction*, Canterbury Press, Norwich, 2008, pp. 62–70.

13 Nowadays we might use the term 'spiritual' for those who are not connected to institutional religion.

you call it God or not, which is different from your everyday life?' Affirmative responses to the Hardy research question asked by a variety of sociologists in Britain over the past 30 years range between 31 per cent and 49 per cent.[14] A survey done in conjunction with the BBC *Soul of Britain* series published in 2000 put the response at 76 per cent, the rise attributed to a greater degree of social permission for such experience.[15] More recently in China, the percentage was 55.9 per cent.[16]

Experience of the 'presence or power, whether [we] call it God or not' is widespread and cross-cultural. It is likely that you or those you know have had some sort of 'encounter'. As you read through Hardy's categories of religious experience, notice what resonates with you or what raises questions.

1 ***Synchronicity and the patterning of events*** – such as 'coincidence', 'things falling into place' or 'working out', unexpected but timely opportunities or meetings with people.
2 ***The presence of God*** – may be described as a 'felt' presence, warmth, light, deep intimate silence, the inner voice of the Holy Spirit and so on.
3 ***Answered prayer.***
4 ***A presence not called God*** – those who reported this were positive about the 'Other' but did not want to use a 'religious' label.
5 ***A sacred presence in nature*** – often associated with, but not limited to, indigenous spiritualities. For example, Australian Aboriginal, New Zealand Māori or North American Indian.
6 ***Experiencing that 'all things are one'*** – for example, a person has an awareness of being at one with the whole of creation, and everything that defines the self as *separate* is momentarily suspended.
7 ***The presence of the dead*** – this does not mean praying to the dead or anything associated with séances or the activities of mediums, but rather being aware of a person who has died,

14 Paul Badham, 'Religion in Britain and China: Similarities and Differences', in *Modern Believing* 49:1, January 2008, pp. 50–8.

15 Pickering, *Spiritual Direction*, p. 67.

16 Badham, 'Religion in Britain and China'.

such as through a dream, or a reassuring vision, or their essence conveyed through light or a fragrance, for example.

8 ***The presence of evil*** – not all spiritual experiences are from God, and we have to be alert to the possibility that a person may have been touched by some force opposed to God, such as an unwelcome presence in a building or place.[17]

To Hardy's original eight categories, the late Gerald May, an experienced psychiatrist and spiritual director,[18] added spiritual experiences such as visions, inspired imagining or gaining a sudden intellectual insight; extra-sensory experiences such as seeing auras, and classic Christian charismatic experiences, which include healing, speaking in tongues, prophecy and words of knowledge.

Some might say that any of these events could be wishful thinking or a matter of interpretation. However, the proof of whether something can be 'classified' as a religious/spiritual experience includes its capacity to be a blessing long after it happens, its unexpectedness, timeliness, relational power, its simplicity and the way it reveals the presence of God in a form we can respond to and recognize.

We notice themes of reconciliation, forgiveness, compassion, grace and creativity ...

... in film, drama and literature, art and sculpture, dance and music. We notice the characters who are 'Christ-like', those situations that model the struggle for justice, acts of sacrifice or service, the power of Love.

We listen to others speaking of their experience of God.

While we might have been brought up not to talk about religion and politics, other faiths and younger people have fewer inhibitions. As we move into our networks outside of the church community, be alert for conversations that include references to faith practices, beliefs or questions.

---

17 If that seems to be the case, seek the assistance of a senior priest and arrange a house blessing or other appropriate ministry. Summarized from Pickering, *Spiritual Direction*, pp. 66–8.

18 Gerald May, *Care of Mind, Care of Spirit*, HarperCollins, New York, 1992, p. 38.

We notice how we feel and what we think about God in response to world events or local tragedy.
Nothing challenges our image of God more than disasters that take the lives of innocents. We hear the 'Why?' questions, and the 'How can God let this happen!' complaints. At such a time we are necessarily propelled into a fresh consideration of how God works in the world.

⌘

The Christchurch earthquakes in 2010–11 brought grief and disruption to many lives in the South Island of New Zealand. In the midst of the trauma and destruction there were some who thought the earthquakes were a judgement on the city and others who thought they were proof that God was indeed dead. But the then Dean of Christchurch Cathedral, Peter Beck, had this to say:

> The earthquake was not an act of God. The earthquake was the planet doing its thing the way the planet does. For me as a Christian, the act of God is in the love and compassion that people are sharing among each other.[19]

Such acts of God included the emergence of the Student Volunteer Army – thousands of young people who went out to clean up affected areas, initially clearing 65,000 tonnes of liquefaction after the 4 September 2010 quake. The group became widely known and its leaders have even been involved in global disaster support and training volunteers. Even now, six years on, the Student Army is an established part of Christchurch life and has changed people's attitude towards the student body for the better.[20]

God-spotting should not be hard once we've learned to see with the eyes of Christ.

⌘

19 See e.g. www.stuff.co.nz/national/christchurch-earthquake/4709342/God-is-in-this-weeping-with-those-who-weep.

20 The Student Volunteer Army continues: www.sva.org.nz/history/.

Going Deeper: God-Spotting

Before you go out of your front door to work or play, ask the Spirit to help you see signs of God's presence in the people and circumstances you encounter.

☺☺ Try Hardy's question for yourself and with family or friends: 'Have you ever had a religious [or spiritual] experience or felt a presence or power, whether you call it God or not, which is different from your everyday life?'

Watch a movie such as *Les Miserables*. Look for the 'Christ-figures' and for themes of redemption justice, self-sacrifice and resurrection.

Next time you visit a care home for the elderly, spend some time sitting with the residents in the lounge and watch the interactions with the staff and visitors. Where can you see God?

As you watch or read the news, see whether you can discover where God might be at work in the world. Notice what catches your attention or touches your heart, and bring this matter to prayer.

Deepening our trust in the Spirit of Jesus

The Christian conviction that God is both One and Three can be challenging, whether we try to 'simplify' it through analogies (e.g. fire/ice/water or three-leafed clovers) or use Augustine's concept of loving community made up of Lover, Beloved and the Love that passes between them. In spiritual direction conversations, I've noticed that people do tend to relate to a particular person of the Trinity at different times in their lives. For me, having an absent father meant that the fatherhood of God was very important for most of my growing up and early adulthood. When I was at a low point and a friend reminded me about Jesus, I went to Him via a Life in the Spirit seminar and the Holy Spirit met me there. Jesus' humanity as well as his divinity continue to take on more and more significance as I witness suffering and death and look for signs of resurrection in the rubble of people's lives. Over the years the Three have become One for me, not just in credal statements but in experience.

- To which person/s of the Trinity do you currently feel most connected?

For the charismatic stream of the Christian faith, the work of the Holy Spirit is emphatically taught and embraced, but many Christians have scant experience of the third Person of the Trinity and little practice in trusting the 'still, small voice' within. Yet Jesus says of the Holy Spirit in John 14:

- I will ask the Father, and he will give you another Advocate/Helper, to be with you for ever (14.16).
- This is the Spirit of truth ... You know him, because he abides with you, and he will be in you (14.17).

- ... the Advocate, the Holy Spirit, whom the Father will send in my name, will teach you everything, and remind you of all that I have said to you (14.26).

The unity among the three persons of the Trinity is beautifully expressed in this last verse – the fullness of the Godhead clearly intends that, through the indwelling of the Holy Spirit, we are to have immediate access to the wisdom, mercy, creativity and love of God, which is ours by adoption as heirs with Christ.

There is a marvellous story of Samuel being sent to Jesse, to find and anoint God's chosen king from among his sons (1 Samuel 16). The drama and mounting tension is palpable as seven hopeful young men are presented to the prophet, but no one is chosen. Finally the youngest son, David, is brought in from the fields and at once the LORD tells Samuel: 'Rise and anoint him; for this is the one' (16.12). We can imagine the consternation of the older brothers and the surprise of the father, but what strikes me is Samuel's absolute trust in the Spirit to lead him through this ordeal. And it is an ordeal, for initially Samuel is afraid to venture near Jesse and tells God so honestly (16.2–3):

> Samuel said, 'How can I go? If Saul hears of it, he will kill me.' And the LORD said, 'Take a heifer with you, and say, "I have come to sacrifice to the LORD." Invite Jesse to the sacrifice, and I will show you what you shall do; and you shall anoint for me the one whom I name to you.'

Notice how honest Samuel is about his fear of Saul. Notice too how practical God is, how specific his instructions. There is no criticism of Samuel's reluctance but rather a reassurance that God *will show him what to do*. And with God's words in his heart and mind, Samuel is able to cope with the lengthy process of elimination until David is found and anointed.

This same specific guidance is seen when Peter is challenged to go to the Gentiles. In Acts 10 there is a detailed account first of the centurion Cornelius and then of the apostle Peter receiving very specific instructions from God. The power and clarity of these visions and words led a willing Peter to go with the men Cornelius had sent to fetch him. When he arrives, it is clear that God's intention is to broaden the blessing of his love to include those who were not Hebrew, and the Holy Spirit is poured out upon the gathered Gentiles even before they are baptized.

The same Spirit who accompanied Samuel on his perilous mission to anoint Saul's successor, and enabled Cornelius and Peter to overcome years of entrenched cultural separation, is available to each of us today, willing to give us the words and practical wisdom we need to do what God gives us to do – if we are practised in honest communication with God and sufficiently still within to receive God's prompts and detailed guidance.

Jesus does not expect us to do immediately what these forebears in the faith did. Instead he builds our capacity to trust him if we invite him into everyday events such as talking to someone we haven't spoken to before, flying for the first time, speaking in front of a group, caring for a little child in an emergency or cooking a simple meal for friends even though we're 'not good in the kitchen'. Each time we do things with the supportive presence of the Spirit of Jesus, we grow in trust, our confidence in Jesus as Emmanuel, 'God with us', increases, and we build a library of personal stories about God's faithfulness.

Years ago I followed God's call to do an MA in Applied Theology in the UK and had to trust God for a faith community, a place to live, work for my husband, a school for our son, the welfare of my elderly mother and inspiration for my ageing grey cells. God took care of it all, even the fee funding shortfall. That comprehensive provision remains a touchstone on my 'trust' journey with Jesus to this day.

Take a few minutes to jot down some of the things you've done as you've relied on the Spirit of Jesus to help you. If this idea is a new one to you, reflect on what you'd like to be able to do and invite the Spirit to be present as you face these opportunities for deepening your trust.

Deepening our trust in the Spirit is a challenge for many in the institutional Church because it gives God room to be God – to be creative, to sing a new song or put new wine into new wineskins.

Yes, there might be conflict, risk and uncertainty, but there will also be excitement, focused service, an increasing sense of connection with each other and our 'neighbours' and the glorious feeling of really doing and being what God is calling us to do and be in this place and time.

If we seriously want to shift our own and the institutional Church's focus from maintenance to mission, we will need to trust God for a lot of things:

- that the Spirit of God that inspired the first-century apostles is available to us today
- that God is already 'out there' at work in the world at large, not confined to the Church or those who profess the Christian faith
- that if we enter our neighbourhoods with humility, as we listen to people's stories with no other agenda than to be the ears, hands and voice of Jesus, we will glimpse the sacred in their lives
- that as we build relationships, opportunities to support, love, serve and share our stories of faith and our love for Jesus will arise naturally
- that as we learn about our communities, the Spirit will help us discern with them how best to respond
- that the grace of God is enough for us, no matter how difficult the situations we face
- that when we partner God in the community, we help to establish church where the people already are, whatever 'church' might look like for them
- that sharing the examples of God's loving presence in the community will enrich the body of Christ and increase enthusiasm for engaging with those 'outside the church'
- that God works according to *kairos* not *chronos*[1] time; it helps to take the long view and not expect immediate 'results' from our patient presence week after week
- that 'nothing will be impossible with God' (Luke 1.37)

1 *Kairos* (Greek) 'the opportune time'; *chronos* (Greek) 'time as we measure it in seconds and minutes etc.'.

- that, as Julian of Norwich would say, 'All shall be well, and all manner of things shall be well.'

⌘

Going Deeper: Deepening Our Trust in the Spirit of Jesus

✍ Look at the list of the things for which we in the Church might need to trust God the Holy Spirit and see what resonates with you *and* what you resist. Both are important to increased self-knowledge! Bring your discoveries to God and then rest in God's love for a while.

🕯 Reflect on your understanding and experience of the Holy Spirit; then, using the *lectio divina* method, spend some time praying with John 14.16:

> 'And I will ask the Father, and he will give you another Advocate, to be with you for ever.'

🕯 If you have never asked to be made aware of/receive the gift of the Holy Spirit, you may want to do this now. The pilot light of the Holy Spirit is burning quietly within you, waiting to be given a new burst of the Breath of life by your petition: 'Fan into flame your Spirit within me, dear Jesus!'

📖 Slowly read the Acts of the Apostles, paying particular attention to the way the Spirit guides the disciples, and praying with small passages that catch your attention.

♥ What are your 'building-trust-in-God' stories?

Theological reflection: the weaving of Scripture, tradition, culture and experience

> Spirit can be known only by spirit – God's Spirit and our spirits in open communion. Spiritually alive, we have access to everything God's Spirit is doing, and can't be judged by unspiritual critics. Isaiah's question, 'Is there anyone around who knows God's Spirit, anyone who knows what he is doing?' has been answered: Christ knows, and we have Christ's Spirit.
>
> *1 Corinthians 2.15–16, The Message*

Asking ourselves 'Where's God in this?' when confronted by something that puzzles, hurts, challenges or comforts us, can build our God-connection and help us develop an appreciation of our faith tradition's relevance to contemporary life in a range of cultural settings. We can engage in theological reflection informally as we go through the day, incorporate it in our evening review practice, or we can approach it in a group setting – or all three!

Theological reflection gives us a window into our inner world through which we can see aspects of ourselves that enhance or inhibit living out our vocation as bearers of the Christ-light. Setting these discoveries in the context of our tradition ensures that we are securely held as we allow ourselves to look at hitherto hidden or 'unacceptable' aspects of our nature or personal story. And rather than assuming God has no part to play in cultures which are 'foreign' to us, be they local pub or strip club, inter-faith gathering or local council meeting, if we find ourselves in such settings, we can ask the 'Where is God in this?' question. God is present, if we stop, look and listen.

Theological reflection is at the core of the well-established Education for Ministry (EFM)[1] programme. In this course we are helped to listen creatively to daily life events, using a particular form of theological reflection with diverse starting points:

- ***Personal experience/action***: for example, 'a slice of life', which can be something that has caught our attention, raised questions, repelled us, touched our heart, challenged our self-image, stretched our comfort zones.
- ***Personal beliefs/values***: noticing when we are challenged by something we've said, done or observed, such as our attitudes towards such issues as LGBTQ rights, our approach to people who are 'different', our inner strengths or weaknesses, our attachments and addictions. It can be disconcerting to face aspects of ourselves revealed by theological reflection, such as being bigoted, judgemental or controlling. But if we trust God's power to transform these less appealing behaviours, they can be redeemed. Similarly, if theological reflection reveals that we have been seduced by materialism and the lure of personal power, the Spirit can help us own this reality and begin to make the transition to a God-centred life in which we hold 'stuff' and status lightly.
- ***Christian tradition***: for example, the nature of God, Scripture and the sacraments, prayer, worship, history, sacred art and music, hymns and songs, the rhythm of the liturgical year, grace, themes of forgiveness, redemption, death and resurrection, the stories of how this tradition came to our land. What does Scripture say? What did Jesus experience? What music evokes a sense of God?

1 'An adult learning course designed to link Christian faith with daily life, and to deepen Christian discipleship', at www.efm.org.nz. For EFM UK, visit www.efm.org.uk. For EFM USA, visit EFM's home base: http://efm.sewanee.edu.

- ***Culture*[2]*/society*:** We move among many cultures at will, using words and behaviours appropriate to each one. So we'll use a certain 'language'[3] within church, when playing sport, eating with friends, in workplaces, preparing food, drinking at the pub, or with hobby groups. Learning the 'language' of those who are 'other' – different from us in whatever way – may not involve actually speaking in a foreign tongue, but does require a sensitivity to what 'other' people value, believe and practise. As we build relationships with people from different cultures, elements such as artwork, music, dance, sacred text, gender roles, gathering protocols, clothing, customs around rites of passage, and the preparation and sharing of food can all offer avenues for shared conversation, including reciprocal story-telling about whether – or how – our faith stories have an impact on our daily lives.

In the left-hand column of the table overleaf is a summary of Killen and de Beer's[4] theological reflection process, which includes a description of how mulling over our experience, including feelings and images, can produce insight. On the right of the table is a succinct example of theological reflection, using a simple 'slice of life' as a starting point.

2 'Culture' is a little like spirituality: there is no standard definition! However, one that is often used is 'the system of shared beliefs, values, customs, behaviours, and artefacts that the members of society use to cope with their world and with one another, and that are transmitted from generation to generation through learning'. From www.umanitoba.ca/faculties/arts/anthropology/courses/122/module1/culture.html.

3 I use 'language' here to encompass communication, customs, beliefs, ways of doing things unique to a particular group.

4 Patricia O'Connell Killen and John de Beer, *The Art of Theological Reflection*, Crossroad, New York, 1994, p. 74, adapted.

'Framework for theological reflection' incorporating 'movement towards insight'	**Starting point: a personal experience**
1 Focusing on some aspect of *experience* allows us to engage with our *feelings*.	I turned up to help distribute lunch at a church function but was told there were enough helpers, though few were visible. I noticed a constriction in my stomach and realized I *felt left out*.
2 Using *metaphor/images* emerging from those feelings, describe *the heart of the matter* – what this event has evoked from your inner life.	When I explored this, the image that came to me was of a little girl hiding in the curtains outside the sitting-room door. I felt a longing to be included ... *the heart of the matter* was that I have felt left out on many occasions and this has shaped my behaviour.
3 Exploring the heart of the matter *in conversation with the wisdom of the Christian heritage* – this may spark *insight*.	When I took this to *prayer*, inwardly I 'saw' Jesus, kneeling on one knee with his arms wide open to welcome me. *God's unconditional love* was reinforced and remains potent. I became more aware of the radical inclusiveness of the gospel and the way this is reflected – or not – in the church today.
4 Identifying from this conversation new truths and meanings for living. *Insight*, if we are willing, leads to *action*.	*Because I know at a deeper level that God will never exclude me*, I am less anxious and don't *need* to worry about being included all the time. I am also more aware of the need to be more welcoming

Each stage of the process is important:

1 Staying with something that has attracted our attention means that we take seriously God's desire to use all sorts of ordinary things to help us notice what's happening in our inner life. Thoughts reflect our current attitudes, values, beliefs; feelings indicate our inner response to an external event. Both are important.
2 Asking 'What's this like?' or 'What metaphor/image comes to mind?' helps us to broaden our perspective, moving from the experience to sensing the impact it might be having on us. This type of open-ended question allows us to be open to creative ways of seeing our motivation, inner thoughts, fears, life positions and so on. The image or metaphor can also point us towards a timely recognition of some inner pain, shame or longing that God is hoping we will recognize, so healing can begin.
3 Once the 'heart of the matter' has popped to the surface of our mind, it is time to ask the Holy Spirit to bring to light aspects of our faith tradition relevant to working with what has been revealed. For example, we might take the heart of the matter to Jesus in prayer; we might talk with a spiritual friend; we might be reminded of a pertinent Scripture, or song or hymn; we might remember a special encounter with someone who helped us know we were loved, as God loves us, without judgement.
4 In the process of exploring these connections with our faith tradition, we may receive an insight, an inner knowing we hadn't expected, something that rings true for us and brings us nearer to living the abundant Christ-life. As we draw the theological reflection to a close, we invite the Holy Spirit to help us apply our learning, to integrate this new knowing into our life and faith practice.

So often we move through life without inviting God into any part of it, unless there is an emergency or a special need for which urgent prayer is sought. The value of taking time to open up an ordinary event to the wisdom of our faith heritage so the light of Christ can shine upon it, is inestimable. Whatever the starting point may be, we can have confidence that through the Holy Spirit, bringing any significant experience to the process of theological reflection helps us to listen more deeply with God and ourselves, our communities and cultures.

⌘

Going Deeper: Theological Reflection

Consider a recent experience in which you encountered someone from another 'culture'.
What was unfamiliar?
How did you feel?
What questions does it raise for you?
Where was God?

Go to your Facebook page (if you have one) and spend five minutes viewing the posts. Use anything that catches your attention as a starting point for theological reflection

Bring to mind a person you know who is on the margins. Allow yourself to spend time with that person either in real life or, if that's not possible, in an imaginative journey that might include key elements of their day, such as going to a community kitchen or finding a place to sleep for the night.
Do some theological reflection on what took place within you, perhaps making some notes in your journal. Remember to ask yourself, 'Where's God in this?'
What insight comes? What might change?

✶ Consider John Trokan's article 'Models of Theological Reflection' (1997) in *Journal of Inquiry and Practice* 1:2, July 2013; http://digitalcommons.lmu.edu/cgi/viewcontent.cgi?article=1032&context=ce. Though written for a university teaching context, Trokan's article helpfully compares several models of theological reflection, affirms its value and offers his own process, which is suitable for *group work*:

- retrieve a significant experience
- retell the experience in story form in small groups
- reframe experiences in the large group
- reconnect the experience to the Christian story
- revision.

- As you do your daily examen tonight, if an incident comes to mind that you want to explore further, go through the theological reflection process so it can be linked more intentionally with the Christian tradition. Notice whether any questions for supervision surface, or whether something emerges that may be taken directly to prayer or unpacked further in spiritual direction.

Naming our natural networks

> He told them another parable: 'The kingdom of heaven is like yeast that a woman took and mixed in with three measures of flour until all of it was leavened.'
> *Matthew 13.33*

Yeast's action is hidden within the flour, and sometimes networks are clandestine from necessity. The 'Underground Railway' was such a network, keeping safe-houses and providing secret routes to enable as many as 100,000 Afro-American slaves to reach freedom in Canada by 1850. Church members such as the Quakers helped ensure the network ran smoothly.[1]

In the twentieth century we know of networks of resistance set up in response to armies of invasion, political or military; countless people who risked everything to help Jews leave places of threat, prisoners to return home and political activists to remain sane.

And now, wherever there is persecution, there will be people of hope, some who are bound to Christ in faith, who will do their utmost to keep alive the Jesus-story and all it means as they work for justice and peace.

Most of us, however, are free to be part of public networks, ordinary groups that provide the sort of social cohesion we often take for granted. Most Thursday mornings I meet a group of friends for a walk. We chat, enjoy a coffee and put the world to rights before we go our separate ways. It's a fluid group but it's part of my natural network, along with the monthly book club, which has been meeting for over 30 years. Both these networks are non-church and informal, but our care for each other has

1 https://en.wikipedia.org/wiki/Underground_Railroad.

developed over the years as we've supported each other through life's challenges.

Our networks extend far beyond those with whom we are currently in contact; relationships forged over many years take on new resonance as pastoral needs arise. In 2015, in the course of a week I had three funerals that linked back to connections made while a tertiary chaplain in the 1990s. As I supported former co-workers grieving the deaths of a beloved adult child, an aged relative and a respected colleague, I was reminded that how we re-present Christ has a lasting impact – for good or ill.

Take a few minutes to reflect on your own experience of relationships made in earlier contexts resurfacing in times of need. What was it that made people feel able to reconnect with you?

Networks often come into their own in times of grief or when a community is torn by tragedy. That is what happened in Christchurch, New Zealand in response to the February 2011 earthquake in which 187 people died and many were left homeless, without food or water. Before the quakes many churches knew little about other churches in their local area, but inspired networking among churches began post-quake, with outstanding results. Two stories will illustrate something of the outpouring of co-operation and effective support for those most in need.

The Rangiora Earthquake Express began two days after the quake. 'This initiative airlifted food [via helicopter] from a rural town north of the city to all points out east ... thanks to the serendipitous linking of two groups of friends representing three different churches.' It was a complex project, 'networking, arranging deliveries, co-ordinating distribution points, drafting press releases ... [the organizers] sensed that folk were being connected not by pure accident but by higher design, and the whole experience was spiritually uplifting.'[2]

2 Melissa Parsons, *Rubble to Resurrection*, Daystar Books, Auckland, NZ, 2014, pp. 27–8.

Christchurch Christian Worship Centre, a medium-sized Assemblies of God church in the worst-hit part of the city, had helped their community after the September 2010 quake. 'Pastor Steve Hira contacted the school (where CCWC ran an after-school care programme), who gave permission to use their hall for a food bank. He called friends and business contacts: support came swiftly from a high school in Palmerston North, his church's national body, Ngāi Tahu (Māori) authority, the local Baha'i Association and Rotary club ...'

As is often God's way, while serving those most in need, those who served are blessed. The helpers came to assist, not to receive, but God ensured they did not leave with empty souls. Here's what happened one day with the CCWC food bank, which

> received supplies from many sources and shared them with other distribution points ... [one day] the need was greater elsewhere and [Pastor] Steve returned to discover the hall was empty ...
>
> [He knew] people would soon be queuing outside. He decided not to get upset and gathered the team in the empty all for a karakia [prayer], inviting the hundred or so volunteers – of all faiths or none – to join in. They asked God to provide for the community and to fill the hall once again. Then, ever practical, Steve got back on the phone. He was in the middle of a call less than an hour later when a church staff member burst in excitedly.
>
> 'Steve, you're not going to believe this!' he yelled.
>
> Steve followed the sound of clapping outside to see a large food-laden transport truck, pulling into the driveway ... and then another ... and another. The cavalcade of vehicles continued and by 6 o'clock that night the hall was again stacked with food. For Steve it was nothing short of a miracle, and he hoped that all who took part in the prayer were touched by witnessing its answer.'[3]

3 Parsons, *Rubble to Resurrection*, pp. 31–2. The CCWC food bank, known and trusted by locals, was a non-official, spontaneous volunteer initiative (extract slightly edited).

- How do you respond to the workers in the above stories sensing that somehow God was present?
  What do you notice about the mix of agencies that responded to help set up the CCWC initiative?
  What is your experience of post-crisis networking?

- Many parts of the world have been hit by damaging extreme weather. How ready is your faith community/congregation to help your community should a natural disaster occur?

⌘

Although some of Jesus' early disciples travelled widely to share the good news, many people heard the Jesus-story from neighbours, family members, friends and others whom they met in the ordinary course of their days. This organic, Spirit-led, courageous model of mission remains relevant today as our *natural networks* provide pathways to engagement with the wider neighbourhood. Whether we are at the school gate, in the doctor's surgery, on the bus or in the queue at a café, we don't wait for someone else to smile or speak, we initiate a connection with a few Spirit-warmed words, without any expectation.

We may do this over and over again for a long time, and risk discouragement and frustration, a bit like the disciples in Luke 5.4–7, whose nets were empty after a night spent trawling the lake. Jesus tells Peter to 'put out into the deep water and let down' his nets again. Jesus asked Peter, asks us all, to persist in the face of disappointment and to move out into the neighbourhood however unenthusiastic or 'out of our depth' we might feel. It is an invitation to trust Jesus, the only One who knows the life circumstances of the people we meet, and the *kairos* moment of their readiness for revelation. God simply asks us to be brave enough to consider *everyone* we meet as someone with whom we may have a spiritual conversation – if the Spirit opens a door.[4]

When Jesus died, it seemed as if all his natural networks died with him. His disciples were scattered, his mission mocked. As

4 'At the same time pray for us as well that God will open to us a door for the word, that we may declare the mystery of Christ' (Colossians 4.3a).

the writer of 'One Solitary Life'[5] emphasized, Jesus wrote no books, didn't travel far, was born in obscurity and died in pain and poverty. Yet with Jesus' resurrection, his Spirit revitalized his disciples, who began to build a network of believers.

This is our task today – to invite the Spirit of Jesus so to revitalize us that we may build networks of disciples who will bring in the kingdom for which God longs, a kingdom where love wins.

⌘

Increasingly the church seeks to engage with those who live in their surrounding neighbourhoods; we may have a profound desire to 'be as Christ in the community', but historically, scant support has been offered to help Christian lay-people engage in winsome conversation about the way Jesus has had an impact on their lives. Setting aside awkward questions focused on personal salvation, Part 2 of this book will focus on our formation as witnesses who can share both the stories of God's grace at work in our lives, and the Jesus-stories relevant to the lives of those we meet in our neighbourhood.

Where do we begin?

On our knees – after that anywhere is God's place, God-space.

If we mapped churchgoers' participation in their natural networks of neighbourhood groups, hobby or sports clubs, service clubs and volunteer agencies, we might be surprised at the range of involvement. If we added those who sit on boards of trustees, mentor the young, enrich the lives of the elderly and seek creative ways of serving those beyond the church, our map might reveal that our local church has networks that extend well beyond its immediate neighbourhood, perhaps even beyond the town or region.

Belonging to networks gives us insight into groups of people who, though not part of a church community, still wrestle with the

5 James Allan Francis, 'One Solitary Life', in *The Real Jesus and Other Sermons*, Judson Press, Philadelphia, PA, 1926.

spiritual questions of meaning and purpose, suffering and justice.

And what about our neighbourhood churches and other faith communities?

How do we feel about initiating connections with people of other religions, of being part of interfaith dialogue or accepting an invitation to attend a festival from another tradition?

⌘

Going Deeper: Naming Our Natural Networks

🕯 Take an A3 piece of paper and make a mind-map[6] (a coloured diagram) of the networks that come to mind as you pray and reflect and listen for God's prompting. Include as many of the different groups/organizations/connections as you can, such as work, church, through partner and children, family of origin, place of birth, your interests, your hobbies, people you meet as you shop or walk in the park, connections made on the internet.

You may be surprised how far your presence permeates a community.

☺☺ With a small group of people from your local church – maybe the staff/wardens/vestry – list the agencies they are already committed to *outside* the church. If this proves to be fun and fascinating, you may want to work it into a service and produce a local map with an estimate of just how many people are within parishioners' personal networks.

The scene is set for empowering your people to witness to God's work in their lives. They don't have to convert or persuade – just tell stories, their own and the stories of Jesus.

---

6 See http://mindmapfree.com/# for a free tool to help you visualize and organize your information into a flexible diagram.

- What agencies need volunteers in your neighbourhood?
- Who in your network is keen on social justice, caring for the poor or homeless and so on?
  How might you get involved or encourage others to offer support, time or resources?

‘PowerPods’: small groups making a difference

> ‘The kingdom of heaven is like a mustard seed that someone took and sowed in his field; it is the smallest of all the seeds, but when it has grown it is the greatest of shrubs and becomes a tree, so that the birds of the air come and make nests in its branches.’
>
> *Matthew 13.31–32*

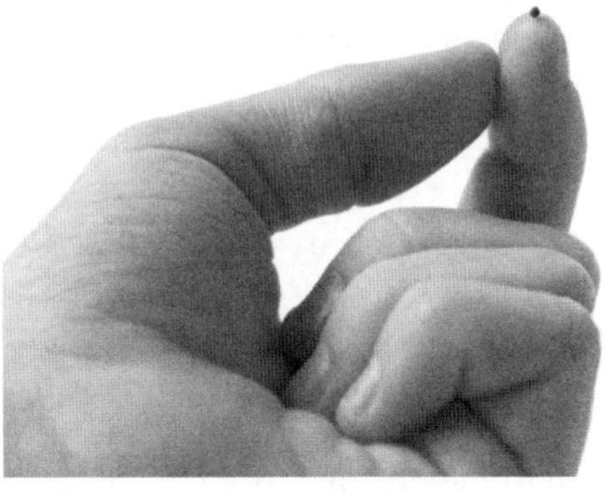

Dandelion seed-bearing parachutes dancing in the breeze may delight us, but it was the mustard seed that served a greater purpose. Jesus used that tiny ‘PowerPod’ to illustrate the growth of the kingdom of God and to remind us that, within ourselves and within our neighbourhood, lies the potential for phenomenal transformation. Even though our love for Jesus is just beginning to light up our lives; even though our intentional movement into our communities might start small – with the right conditions and care, small beginnings can produce something substantial enough to support others in their own becoming and make a genuine and long-lasting difference.

In countless places around the world, little groups of Christians are making a significant contribution to the lives of people in their communities and beyond, with Spirit-led projects that reflect one or more of the Anglican marks of mission.[1] William Temple's words, 'Church is the only society on earth that exists for the benefit of non-members', encourage us to listen to God in our neighbourhood, alert for need, persistent in prayer, ready to engage with the community in practical projects to make a difference for good.

Richard Randerson's book *Engagement 21: A Wake-up Call to the 21st Century Church in Mission*[2] gives an overview of more than a hundred 'Green shoots' projects through which local churches in New Zealand engage their communities. These range from 'God-talk' gatherings, community houses, language classes, building a Habitat for Humanity house using a church car park and the support of seven parishes, released prisoner housing, community gardens and ongoing protection of threatened local environments.

The opportunities are endless, and so are the needs of those around us.

Imagine yourself in a PowerPod of Christians *active* in your neighbourhood – resourced by waiting on God in contemplative prayer, listening deeply to Scripture and each other, committed to deepening your awareness of God's work beyond the church, learning more about yourselves, motivated by the love of Jesus and your love for the people around you …

Imagine little PowerPods of faith dotted here and there among the concrete of the urban landscape, pushing up and bringing beauty into grey days and busy streets …

Imagine that, with the blessing and ongoing support of your church, you would:

---

1 Bonds of Affection-1984 ACC-6, p. 49, Mission in a Broken World-1990 ACC-8, p. 101; www.anglicancommunion.org/identity/marks-of-mission.aspx.

2 Bishop Richard Randerson's book is available at randersonjr@paradise.net.nz as a PDF.

- form into pairs, trios or small groups, joining others who have a common desire to get to know people in your immediate neighbourhood
- listen to God together, and act only as the Spirit leads
- go God-spotting, looking for what God is already doing, alert for signs of love and suffering, peace and hope, struggle and reconciliation
- begin to build intentional friendships with those in your neighbourhood whoever they are, listening to people's lives and singing your God-song as the Spirit enables
- be at the forefront of local mission
- hear more about community needs and, in conversation and in prayer, begin to discover how God might want to address these needs
- work alongside others in the community (and with anyone else from your church who feels drawn) to enable a project to come to fruition.

The process of forming such PowerPods will emerge as your church unfolds a vision of moving effectively into the community, at the bidding of the Spirit. Of course, some of this movement is already happening informally as members of congregations serve on all sorts of boards and agencies. But what is different is the intentionality of these PowerPods and their commitment both to our own spiritual formation as disciples of Jesus, and our own willingness to sharing our God-stories in the neighbourhood, bearing witness to the grace of God and gifting our faithful presence to a particular community.

Let's dream for a minute about how a few sample PowerPod groups, led by the Spirit, might begin to connect with people 'on the margins':

- Two older women living in pensioner housing begin to visit their neighbours, bringing home-made baking and time to listen over a cup of tea. Over time their example encourages others to reach out to those around them. Feeling safer and less lonely, the older women's neighbours are willing to accept an invitation to have lunch once a month at a drop-in café run by their church.

- Three teenage boys at a local school are worried about the bullying of younger boys and decide to try to get alongside those affected. They speak to the guidance counsellor about their concerns and help establish a peer-led anti-bullying patrol and education programme to keep students safe.
- Two Christian immigrant couples with young children meet for a meal every week. They have a heart for others who, like them, are without family support in an unfamiliar country. They become aware of other immigrants – a Muslim couple and a Hindu couple living nearby, whom they invite to share common concerns over a meal. Over time they all learn about their respective cultures and religious observance. Matters of faith become a regular part of their dinner conversation.

Spend some time bringing to God your own neighbourhood and networks.
What moves you as you listen to God in the silence of your heart?

⌘

Sometimes projects remain on a small scale, answering a very local need and lasting for a season before being discontinued. But sometimes projects 'grow like topsy', and when that happens it's like standing back in awe to see what God does with the 'mustard seed' planted in faith. The following four projects all started *small*:

- ***The Church of the Saviour*** in Washington, DC was founded in 1947 by Gordon and Mary Cosby and seven others. It 'interprets the call to discipleship as the interweaving of two journeys in community – an inward journey, growing in love of God, self and others, and an outward journey, helping to restore some part of God's creation'. Now a network of some 40 churches and organizations, it provides a medical centre, retreat centre, post-prison release and social justice projects, and diverse, inclusive expressions of church. Its members practise contemplative prayer, personal and corporate accountability, and support each other as they grow in their love for Jesus.[3]

3 http://inwardoutward.org/the-church-of-the-saviour/our-story.

- ***A Rocha*** (Portuguese: the 'rock') is the Christian Conservation Network. In 1983 Peter and Miranda Harris and Leslie and Wendy Batty and their young families moved from Merseyside, where Peter had been in Anglican parish ministry, to Portugal. The first field study centre and bird observatory on the Ria de Alvor opened in 1986. 'International interest gradually increased and in 2000, after A Rocha had begun work in Lebanon, France, Kenya and Canada, A Rocha International was formed. Currently A Rocha has national organizations in 19 countries responding to the critical loss of biodiversity through community-based conservation projects, residential field study centres, site-based projects and wider advocacy.'[4]
- ***The Bishop's Action Foundation*** was founded in 2005 in Taranaki, New Zealand. It acts as a catalyst, working with existing and new groups to improve services and build community well-being. Set up by the Bishop of Taranaki, now Archbishop Philip Richardson, in collaboration with a handful of key advisers and strategists, BAF resources programmes for children affected by grief and loss, mentoring of disadvantaged children, and parenting programmes. It is involved in researching affordable housing pathways for low-income families, the needs of rural elderly and the relationship between spirituality and well-being, and is active in helping the church maximize its resources in changing communities.
- ***Te Aroha Noa*** (Māori: 'unlimited love') is an 'innovative family/whanau and community development organization with an underpinning Christian kaupapa [principles/values]. It is based in a lower socio-economic and multicultural suburb of Palmerston North, New Zealand. Initiated in 1989 by a small group of local Baptists, it has grown over the following 20 years to serve the western suburbs communities and the regions around Palmerston North. Some 63 staff and 150 volunteers provide innovative community development services and initiatives such as: HIPPY, First Steps Adult Learning Community, Aerobics and Gym, Craft Group, Counselling and Therapy, Violence Free Community, Family/Whanau

4 For further information see www.arocha.org/en/overview.

Development, Practice Research and Teaching and Early Childhood Education.'[5] Enabling God-talk and respecting participants' spirituality are woven into the fabric of this effective community agency.[6]

Remember the mustard seed – nothing is impossible with God.

⌘

Going Deeper: PowerPods

- Imagine the Good Samaritan story set somewhere in *your own neighbourhood.*
  Take a moment to get a sense of someone slumped in a sorry heap, avoided by passers-by until some unlikely person stops, kneels, touches, offers water and then helps them towards a place of shelter. What might this say to you about your own context and your own resistance?
  If you were writing this today, who might have 'walked by on the other side'/stopped to help?
- What small PowerPods or their equivalent are you already part of/aware of in your own church/among your own friends or family?
- What other Christian-based agencies do you know of that started small but grew like the mustard seed?
- As you mentally scan your neighbourhood, is there already something that attracts your attention – that invites you to further prayer and investigation? Is there already someone who might share the same focus?

---

5 www.tearohanoa.org.nz/who-we-are.html. HIPPY: 'Home Interaction Programme for Parents and Youngsters' (abridged).

6 See CEO Bruce Maden's paper in 'Further reading' for an insight into how spirituality is addressed at Te Aroha Noa.

PART 2

Spiritual conversation: becoming witnesses

'But you will receive power when the Holy Spirit has come upon you; and you will be my witnesses in Jerusalem, in all Judea and Samaria, and to the ends of the earth.'
Acts 1.8

Introduction

> I've preached you to the whole congregation,
> I've kept back nothing, GOD – you know that.
> I didn't keep the news of your ways a secret, didn't keep it to myself.
> I told it all, how dependable you are, how thorough.
> I didn't hold back pieces of love and truth for myself alone.
> I told it all, let the congregation know the whole story.
>
> *Psalm 40.9–10, The Message*

Stories connect us – to our own experience, to family, friends and community, and to our heritage. They have the power to bring a past event into the present moment and make it live again. They help us discover significant truths about life and well-being, about meaning and belonging to something or Someone greater than ourselves. As I've got older, part of the joy of growing in Christ has come through engagement with the stories of Scripture: stories of God's people as they tried to live in covenant relationship with the God who accompanied them through the wilderness of disobedience and doubt; stories of Jesus' unique personhood and passion; stories of the work of the Holy Spirit empowering ordinary people to share the gospel across the known world. Such stories anchored me in the lived experience of faith, where the 'rubber hits the road', and continue to keep me close to Jesus to this day. Such stories both enable and inform our witness, as we shall explore shortly. But let's begin with a recent and personal story.

John and the TV show that touched his soul

A few months ago, my husband John was watching one of his favourite genealogy programmes, *Who do you Think you Are?* In this particular episode, the actress Rebecca Gibney discovered that her great-grandfather had been one of the voluntary militia who invaded the settlement of Parihaka in 1881. Fifty years before Gandhi famously used passive resistance in his people's struggles in India, two Māori prophets, Tohu and Te Whiti, influenced by Christian teaching and their own determination and principles, encouraged their people to pull up surveyors' pegs and plough up roads made by settlers hungry for more land. When over 2,000 troops arrived to take the peaceful town by force, they were met by the children, sitting in the way, singing songs. The outcome was predictably dire: innocent people were violated and imprisoned without trial. The town was brought to its knees.

Rebecca's story was unique because for the first time, a descendant of someone *directly* involved in the invasion and sacking of Parihaka was meeting descendants of those *directly* harmed. Tears traced tracks down the faces of the kuia[1] present as the kaumatua told their story candidly, without blame or bitterness, true to the Christian principles of the village's founders. They were able – literally – to hold Rebecca in love as she listened, knowing her ancestor, whose photograph she'd been asked to bring with her, had been among those who destroyed the lives of their ancestors. As the story came to a close, Rebecca stood and spoke of her 'blindness', of 'now seeing' the injustice and the struggle more clearly; and then, as Māori custom calls for a waiata (song) to follow a korero (speech), Rebecca chose that most fitting hymn, 'Amazing Grace'. Not surprisingly, tears rolled down the faces of those participating in this act of reconciliation – and down our faces too at the grace enfolding them all.

The day after seeing the programme, John started to tell others about what he had experienced and how it had touched him. His eyes would fill with tears as he recounted the grace flowing between those who could so easily have been cruel and condemn-

1 Kuia (coo-ee-ah): respected female Māori elder; kaumatua (coe-mah-two-ah): respected male Māori elder.

ing and Rebecca, who was so profoundly moved. It was clear to those listening to him that something special had happened, that he wanted others to get close to that unique moment of grace and healing. This story had moved him to the core and he found himself *witnessing to others*, sharing his 'God-moment' naturally and beautifully.

⌘

As witnesses we speak of what we know from our own experience. That is our role initially – not to persuade or even try to explain but simply to say what we saw, heard, felt, touched, tasted or intuited. As witnesses we don't need to try to steer a conversation towards a moment when we can 'introduce' God; instead we trust that there will come a natural opportunity to share something of our God-story when the Holy Spirit opens the door.[2] Our responsibility and joy is to listen to the feisty, confident or fractured songs of those we meet and then sing our own, as the Spirit gives us voice and the courage and the grace we need. There is no doubt that God's Spirit can make bold the timid and put words into the mouths of the unlikely messenger. What God did for Moses and others can be done with and for us as well, when we least expect it.

Being so moved by a God-moment that people seek to share it with others is a common dynamic in Scripture. For example, in chapter 5 of Mark's Gospel we read the drama of the Gerasene demoniac: a deranged man is freed from all that deprived him of humanity, pigs die controversially and witnesses are torn between awe and fear. At its centre is Jesus, whose authority, compassion and focused presence bring the man to a still point in which he knows himself healed. The story could well have ended there, but with the man's dignity and sanity restored, Jesus gives him something wonderful to do:

---

2 'Devote yourselves to prayer, keeping alert in it with thanksgiving. At the same time pray for us as well that God will open to us a door for the word, that we may declare the mystery of Christ, for which I am in prison, so that I may reveal it clearly, as I should' (Colossians 4.2b–4).

> As he was getting into the boat, the man who had been possessed by demons begged him that he might be with him. But Jesus refused, and said to him, '*Go home to your friends, and tell them how much the Lord has done for you, and what mercy he has shown you.*' And he went away and began to proclaim in the Decapolis how much Jesus had done for him; and everyone was amazed.
> *Mark 5.18–20, emphasis mine*

Jesus very specifically sends the healed man to *tell others* – to be a witness to the power and wonder of God's love. Not only would the man and the listeners be blessed with each retelling, over time his story would percolate through the Decapolis, the multicultural region in which he lived. Jesus asked the healed man to sing his God-song in a context in which Jewish belief in a supernatural God left them marginalized, and where the majority of people, strongly influenced by Greek and Roman culture, held beliefs similar to contemporary humanism; that is, that progress for humanity lay not through divine revelation, but in the aspirations, minds, education and reasoning of the human being.

- But what of the other witnesses, those who watched as pigs drowned, swineherds panicked and the power of God was made fearfully visible? What story did they choose to tell? Would they report things that affected *others* or reveal things that affected them? Or would they choose, as some witnesses do, to remain silent?
- I am convinced that God is at work among us, that there are stories of God's goodness stored in our hearts and minds. Yet how many of us share these stories with those we know?
- How many of us actually talk about our God-moments, the touches of grace, answers to prayer, moments of deep peace, timely support in difficult situations, God-given encounters and chances to serve?
- How many of us remain silent?
- Why?

🕯 Take a moment to think about a response to that question before moving on.

There are many reasons we don't engage in God-talk:

- historical or cultural restriction on 'religion' as a 'suitable topic' for conversation means that we have little experience of God-talk being a 'normal' part of daily life
- we're embarrassed because of the way far-right Christians are portrayed in the media and we don't want to be tarred with the same brush
- we don't know how to find the words to explain part of our life that is a mystery
- we have nothing to say because we haven't noticed what God is up to in our lives
- we discount our God-moments because we think we might be imagining them
- we don't tell others because we think it would be like 'casting pearls before swine' (Matthew 7.6)
- natural shyness or introversion makes it hard to share things close to our hearts.

What stories will we tell? What song will we sing?
Or will we be a silent witness?
Will the truth of what God means to us emerge only after our death – or not at all?

⌘

Witnessing through story-sharing naturally develops:

- a commitment to listen FIRST; only then can we begin to share our own truth in a way that does not detract from the other's experience but serves to establish empathy and enable further conversation
- being prepared to talk about aspects of our lives that might resonate with the other person
- being able to put words around how God has met us in those situations and continues to uphold us
- being familiar with Jesus-stories that reflect common human feelings and experiences

- o being able to talk about what Jesus offers: an ongoing companionship sustained by Trinitarian love.

So in this second part of the book we focus on what Jesus gives us to do – go out into the community, practise holy listening, and witness to God's grace by singing our God-song among those we meet.

With media focus on the controversial, the salacious and the divisive, the public are more likely to hear stories about negative aspects of the Christian faith, rather than the Church and Christian's 'core business' – transforming lives and communities through Christ. *We* have to tell those stories or they won't be told. According to the scriptural imperative echoing through psalms, stories and tradition, we are to witness to what God is doing in and around us.

The choice to remain silent is not an option for us if we are followers of the Way.

Building relationships that empower: respectful engagement

Jesus empowered people by attending to them with his whole being and, in a divine form of tough love, letting them make their own choices. He offered people healing and spiritual growth: the former was welcomed, the latter often rejected as old habits, status and priorities were challenged. His Spirit continues this work in and through us as *we engage with others respectfully*, taking nothing from their personhood, building up their sense of worth and modelling the transformation that Christ works in each of us if we are willing.

Building empowering relationships with others begins with some work on our *interpersonal communication skills and use of power*. In our role as priests, pastoral workers or in our families or workplaces, we can empower or weaken others. We might think we have no personal influence as we try to assist other people or listen to their stories, but the 'dog collar' gives us power, our 'official title' or role gives us power, things like age and education give us power, and so on. If we are unaware of this power in our pastoral encounters, not only are we blind, we are dangerous.

> In the aftermath of the 2016 Orlando massacre in which 49 people attending a gay bar in Florida were murdered, further anguish for at least one of the families arose, because they were unsure if they could find a minister and a church for their gay son's funeral. This was in spite of their son being a regular churchgoer and committed Christian.[1]

1 See CNN interview with Shane Tomlinson's parents: http://edition.cnn.com/videos/us/2016/06/17/shane-tomlinson-parents-rememer-their-son-sot-lemon-tonight.cnn/video/playlists/who-are-the-orlando-shooting-victims.

Power, vested in the ministers of the gospel by those who look to them for support, can be dreadfully misused. Many of us have heard such stories, often identified as the tipping point for a decision to walk away from organized religion, even from God. We'd all like to think that we would never be so lacking in compassion, but I suspect there have been times when we've witnessed or done something that has been hurtful to others in some way, however unintentionally.

- How does this last sentence resonate with your experience of pastoral ministry?

However inept we are at times, our intention as people of God is to try to build others up, include those on the margins, encourage the meek to speak for themselves, stand alongside the unwell as they find their way to healing, offer companionship as newcomers settle into our community, and advocate for the aged or imprisoned. It's challenging and difficult, but it is of God.

As we move into the neighbourhood, we don't go as health professionals, family members, financial or legal advisers, counsellors, social workers, building inspectors or door-to-door salespeople. Valid though these services are, we have something entirely different to offer. Remember Peter, who said in Acts 3.6: 'I have no silver or gold, but *what I have* I give you', and went on to heal in Jesus' name.

As ministers of the gospel we offer our loving presence, our firm belief in the transformative power of the love of God and, if the Spirit leads us, a willingness to pray aloud or in our hearts according to what fits the person's need and their receptivity to prayer. Leonard Sweet said: 'Insects crawl, fish swim, birds fly and humans pray.'[2] If we are respectful, have taken the time to listen well, have built up rapport and have a sense of how we might pray, it's unlikely that people will refuse the chance to have someone pray *with* them. And *with* is the operative word – for that word conveys not 'power over' but 'being with'. We never

2 On Twitter: Leonard Sweet @lensweet 8.6.2013.

pray alone: Jesus prays with us through his Spirit (Romans 8.26–27). We can ask the other person, 'What shall we pray for?' The more we can encourage people to express their needs, to offer their own prayers with our support, the more we empower them to develop both the spiritual practice of intercession and petition[3] and a closer relationship with God and with other people.

⌘

Although the following might seem a surprising inclusion, if we are to empower others, it's helpful to know what might be going on when communication breaks down. When relationships run into trouble, it's likely that one of five common interpersonal dynamics is at work.

- ***Parallel process*** occurs when someone tells us about an issue or situation that directly or indirectly corresponds to something in our own life. For example, Nick, a pastoral worker, who has just been recalled for further tests following a recent colonoscopy, visits Ted, who's anxious about his imminent surgery for bowel cancer; Mary tells Revd Molly she is worried about post-natal depression, not knowing that Molly's daughter-in-law is dealing with the same issue.

  Instead of being fully present to the situation, we risk being distracted by the parallel, even to the point of switching off or taking over the conversation to share our experience.

- ***Projection*** happens when, instead of acknowledging personal issues, we may unconsciously project them on to someone else so we don't have to face our own disturbing or embarrassing traits. For example, a controlling family member accuses others of trying to control him; a parishioner whom you've noticed is very rude to others complains about your rudeness to her.

3 Intercession: praying for others; petition: praying for ourselves.

- ***Transference*** happens when we react strongly to something about a person that, at an unconscious level, evokes feelings and memories about an earlier relationship – good or bad. When this transference happens, we respond to the other person as if she were our angry teacher, overbearing older sibling or dearly loved granny, instead of relating to her as she actually is. This can happen very easily in pastoral encounters, especially if we have not done the inner work that would help us recognize our points of vulnerability. For example, I discovered that when working with families preparing a funeral for an elderly parent, I envied the sharing of stories by the siblings, for whom the vigil was a time of grace and strengthening of family bonds. As an only child, I recognized this longing within me and took it to supervision so it would not get in the way of my ability to enable the siblings' process.

- ***Counter-transference*** occurs when those who respond 'buy' into the person's behaviour. For example, in the scenario above, the siblings might have felt obliged to include me, or been annoyed at my deep interest in the stories they were sharing and my staying with them longer than I needed to. In other words, they were affected by what I was doing and reacted.

- ***Dysfunctional triangulation***[4] happens when, instead of dealing directly with a situation or person, we talk to a third party about it, trying to get them on our side, do our work, even 'fire our bullets' for us. Clergy, pastoral workers and caregivers are particularly at risk of buying into this pattern, because we want to 'help' and are often sought out for 'advice'. Once we learn how to minimize dysfunctional triangulation, benefits accrue to the other parties involved as they learn how to be more direct about what matters to them, and to us because it takes a lot less energy and time.

4 For an interesting clip about this particular process, originally addressed by Murray Bowen in his Family Systems theory, watch www.youtube.com/watch?v=47rDdeSPTGs.

Look at the first two cases below to see what I mean. In each case you are 'B':

▸ **Scenario 1**

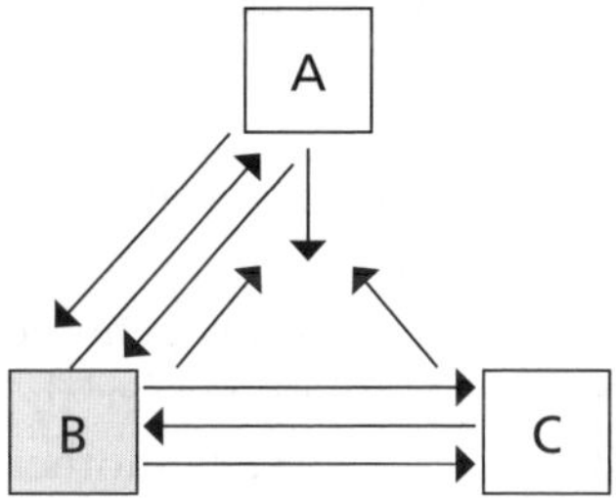

A comes to B to talk about an issue with C.
B listens and offers to talk to C about what has upset A.
B talks to C who decides he will apologise to A.
B tells A that C wants to apologise.
A asks B to arrange a meeting with C.
B does so and offers to be there.
A, B and C meet and peace is made.

▸ **Scenario 2**

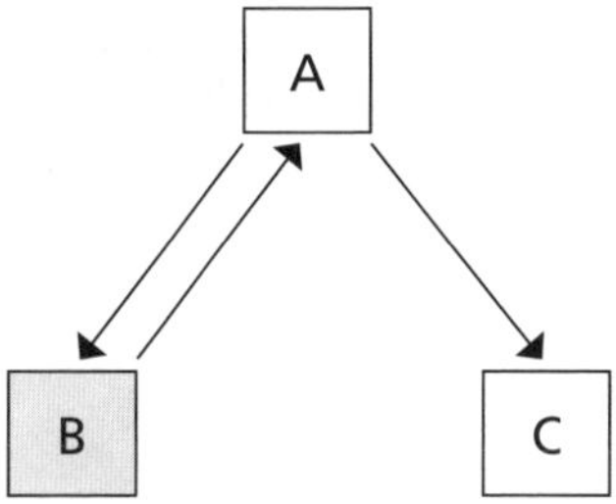

A comes to B to talk about C.
B listens and helps A explore his options.
A goes to C directly and talks about what is troubling him.

Noticing this pattern in our own interactions will help us assist others when they are caught in unhealthy triangulation.

▸ **Scenario 3**

The goal is for us all to be able to attend to issues in a timely way *directly* with those who are involved, drawing on the wisdom of the only third party we shall ever need: the ever-present compassionate Helper, who is always waiting to be invited into our lives.

⌘

Being aware of 'how we tick' and what 'pushes our buttons' makes us more authentic in our relationships, and so does learning to take responsibility for our own 'stuff'. The story of Adam and Eve in Genesis is a classic example of people not taking responsibility for their own behaviour! In Genesis 3.12–13, when questioned by God about his awareness of being naked, Adam blames Eve and Eve blames the serpent!

When I've talked with people who've been wronged in some way, most do not seek 'reparation' – they simply want people to own up to what they have done, to be honest and show genuine remorse. Wrongdoers who shift blame on to others hinder the process of resolution and forgiveness. But as Jesus says, 'If another disciple sins, you must rebuke the offender, and *if there is repentance*, you must forgive' (Luke 17.3). Restorative justice[5] is at the heart of this process: through skilled mediation, volatile emotions are safely expressed; ideally the wrongdoer is enabled to face his/her behaviour and makes what we'd call a 'confession'; the wronged person tells the wrongdoer what impact his/her transgression has had; and an offer of forgiveness may, through the grace of God, be made and accepted.

⌘

Going Deeper: Building Relationships that Empower

- Spend some time watching the television news and see what you can learn about the use/abuse of power in the way people are interviewed or treated. Then transfer your attention to those with whom you live, work or minister. Notice how power is used by them – and by you.

5 See www.rpiassn.org/practice-areas/what-is-restorative-justice.

- Ask for the protection of the Holy Spirit and then identify a time when you felt disempowered. If what comes to mind is painful, invite God to guide your reflection in the best way possible – it may be wise for you to do this work with someone you trust alongside you. You may want to journal, sketch, or shout your thoughts as you recall how this situation unfolded and the impact it has had. If what you have recalled requires further exploration, perhaps with professional support, give yourself that time and know that, although it may be hard work, it will be for your healing. When you feel emotionally strong, ask God to help you see how this experience might inform your pastoral ministry.
- Pay close attention to your pastoral interactions over the next two weeks. Notice whether prayer is part of your natural connection with those you meet, what you say, how you say it, and the other person's level of involvement.
- Consider the section on common unhelpful interpersonal dynamics: parallel process, projection, transference, counter--transference and dysfunctional triangulation. Spend some time reflecting on each one in relation to your own experience.

Listening to our communities

... with all humility and gentleness, with patience, bearing with one another in love, making every effort to maintain the unity of the Spirit in the bond of peace. There is one body and one Spirit, just as you were called to the one hope of your calling, one Lord, one faith, one baptism, one God and Father of all, who is above all and through all and in all.

Ephesians 4.2–6

When I think about the word 'community', what first comes to mind is a quiet, early, weekday communion service when up to a dozen of us gather to share the Eucharist and the silence with our Bishop. Over the last 17 years, some members have died or grown more frail; others have felt the effects of divorce, disappointment or depression, but week by week we gather and, for a precious half hour, give form to the 'body of Christ' as we are nourished by word and sacrament.

In his book, *Living Faithfully*, Bishop John Pritchard comments on two distinct ways of understanding community. An example of the first would be the 7 a.m. service described above: it's a community whose members know and care for each other deeply; there's a comfortable predictability in both role and ritual, so people can feel safe and just 'be' with God, like sitting in front of the fire with an old friend.

The second way of understanding community, however, is less

predictable, more dynamic, creative, exciting and scary! This is '*communitas*'[1] which, according to Pritchard:

> focuses on a task outside of the group so that building community isn't an end in itself, which can lead to staleness, but a by-product of another intentional activity. It's when the church is committed to serving the wider community that the special belonging of *communitas* occurs by happy accident.

Church communities ideally embody inclusiveness as they gather for worship and to form disciples. But the church is really energized, Pritchard concludes, 'only when it is focused beyond itself, when it's missional',[2] when we move into the unknown, led out of our comfort zones by the Spirit. Two stories illustrate what can happen when people are 'as Christ' in their neighbourhoods.

> Ron and his wife had belonged to churches in various cities, serving on committees and even going on mission trips. They had been very busy but rarely felt they were truly following and joining with Jesus in their whole lives ... [One day] instead of having a beer on his own on the back deck, Ron headed towards the front door ... He'd been getting to know people in his neighbourhood and it was time to go deeper. With some beers and folding chairs he made for the front lawn and within half an hour or so, a bunch of neighbours was enjoying cold beer and conversation. The gathering gave Ron a glimpse of what church could be.

> An experienced Canadian pastor, Karen, started to change the patterns of her life, as she became more and more certain that Jesus was calling her to re-enter her neighbourhood and be with the people ... over the years she has opened her home and welcomed others to live with her; she hosts a monthly Soup Night

1 Apart from its specific anthropological use, *communitas* (Latin) means an unstructured community in which people are equal.

2 John Pritchard, *Living Faithfully*, SPCK, London, 2013, pp. 126–7. The distinction between community and *communitas* was originally explored in Victor Turner, *The Ritual Process*, Aldine, Chicago, 1969.

and invites the neighbourhood to gather to share food and life stories around the table. Karen has no trouble seeing God at work and sensing how the Spirit is forming something quite different from the church ministry she had maintained for so many years.[3]

Karen and Ron were able to connect with their neighbours because they listened to others well. Instead of promoting themselves and their own opinions, they were fortified by prayer, patience and a passion for hearing the human heart, and recognized that hospitality enables relationship. As they paid loving attention to those they met, relationships and *communitas* began to flourish and God's presence was revealed. Their experience, and that of many others, reveals that being 'missional' requires preparation, the right attitude, presence and hospitality!

Preparation

We do our best to make sure that we have done our homework as we prepare to move with Jesus into our neighbourhoods. This will include:

- spending time in listening prayer
- praying for the grace we need; for example, being honest with God about any misgivings or excitement is important so that we are neither too anxious nor over-enthusiastic!
- covering the material in the first half of this book, ideally in the context of a small group or PowerPod and with the support of our church's commitment to forming disciples and witnesses
- making a commitment with our PowerPod partner/s to regular prayer together
- familiarizing ourselves with the neighbourhood, such as major industry/business, schools, housing, economic well-being, ethnic mix, cafés and public facilities, and recent census demographics
- praying before setting out – that the Holy Spirit will prepare the way, open doors and give us the words that fit the context

3 Alan Roxburgh, *Joining God, Remaking Church, Changing the World*, Morehouse, New York, 2015, pp. 38–9 (abridged).

- taking with us some small tokens of our faith; for example, a holding cross, a little booklet of scriptural comfort such as those provided by the Bible Society – keep these in your pocket with the aim of sharing them *if the Spirit prompts you.*

Attitude

When Jesus sent out the 70 disciples (Luke 10.4) he specifically told them to travel lightly, without the security of money, food or a change of clothes, *trusting* instead in the grace of God and ready to share the good news of the kingdom of God among them.

The manner in which we approach people beyond the church will determine whether or not open, respectful conversations can flourish. Jesus was *gentle* among the sick and suffering, and didn't 'put down' the marginalized or those who were genuine seekers after the true nature of God as love. The people who were in conversation with him would have experienced his focused presence and felt completely accepted as they were. We too are called to be courteous in our dealings with others rather than confrontational or unkind; we affirm people's worth, listen to their stories, offer any comments with kindness, and leave them more hopeful, rather than feeling diminished. As Paul writes:

> Use your heads as you live and work among outsiders. Don't miss a trick. Make the most of every opportunity. Be gracious in your speech. The goal is to bring out the best in others in a conversation, not put them down, not cut them out.
> *Colossians 4.5–6, The Message*

Pre-conversion, the apostle Paul had persecuted and imprisoned Christians. Post-conversion, the Holy Spirit enabled Paul to treat people with diplomacy and respect, meeting them 'where they were at' without compromising his own faith (1 Corinthians 9.19–23), and acknowledging their efforts to connect with the sacred beyond themselves (Acts 17.22–28).[4]

---

4 A particularly relevant approach when speaking with those who are 'spiritual but not religious'.

If cobwebs of ecclesiastical superiority *still* cling to our thinking as we head off into our neighbourhoods, we won't make any headway, particularly in a multicultural context. Lesslie Newbigin approached his 30 years of missionary work in India by first of all recognizing that *he was the outsider*. As such he knew he:

> needed to listen to and learn the cultures of that vast country's peoples. He would do this by sitting in villages with local religious leaders and they would read each other's sacred texts ... Because he was constantly compelled to read the gospel from the perspective of the other ... he was driven ever more deeply into the study of the Scriptures to relearn what was there.[5]

And so we enter the neighbourhood with *humility*, ready to learn, respectfully engaging with what is important to the people we meet. *We make no assumptions* but listen to what others have to say about their lives, about what *they* hold dear. We build on the things we hold in common rather than fight over the things we view differently. We restrain ourselves from being nosey, trying to fix things, rushing to fill a pause or saying 'I know how you feel.'[6] We avoid judging others or interrupting; instead we listen.

Like Newbigin, we may be challenged to look at our own sacred texts and practices from another's perspective and in doing so, go deeper into what God might be saying to us in this new context.

Listening to people's observations about the Church and what *we* value, we're likely to encounter issues that have diverted the Church from its core mission and tied up its resources for far too long (e.g. homosexuality, women's ordination or worries about maintenance), and negative attitudes towards the Church and its members (e.g. hypocrisy, moral failures of leadership, irrelevance). While the focus of this book is on simple story-sharing rather than on apologetics,[7] we still need to have done our own thinking and

5 Alan Roxburgh, *Missional: Joining God in the Neighbourhood*, Baker Books, Grand Rapids, MI, 2011, p. 35.

6 Although we may have had similar feelings, we do not share the context, background, personality and so on of the other person and so we *cannot* know how they feel.

7 Christian apologetics is the theological discipline of conducting a reasoned explanation and defence of key doctrines.

praying about such challenges because our position will affect our capacity to be present to others' experiences. As Peter writes:

> But in your hearts, set apart Christ as Lord. Always *be prepared* to give an answer [apologia] to everyone who asks you for the reason for the hope that you have, but do this with gentleness and respect, keeping a clear conscience.
> *1 Peter 3.15–16*

If we are not prepared, we risk defaulting into defensiveness, trying to enforce our viewpoint at the other's expense, even becoming angry and damaging the very relationships we are trying to build.[8]

🕯 To the list of potentially difficult topics of spiritual conversation, add any that have particular relevance for you. For each one, reflect on what you believe and see if you can come to a position you can express 'with gentleness and respect, keeping a clear conscience'.

Presence

In prisons, care homes for the elderly, hospitals, industry, armed forces, sports teams, schools, universities and in the wider community, chaplains unobtrusively serve at the 'coal face' where faith meets the doubts and questions, the celebration and the suffering of ordinary people in ordinary time. Chaplains offer the priceless ministry of *faithful presence*, *confidential listening* and *a still, sacred space* when all around is frantically busy or overwhelmed by unexpected tragedy.

> Defence Force chaplain Revd Capt. Paul Stanaway and his colleague, chaplain Kevin Brophy, were on hand at the morgue set up at the Burnham Military Base, after the February 2011 Christchurch earthquakes, helping where they could. The Defence Force had reassured the families of the victims they would not be left alone and Paul recalls walking slowly among

8 For more on challenging spiritual conversations, see pp. 99–105.

the containers, stopping every now and again 'to pray, think, even sing, very, very quietly ... It was discrete. But for me, the Presence of God was powerful.'

Paul recalled one of the most difficult post-mortems: 'When a mother and baby were brought in, a silence fell in the room, as many of the soldiers and DVI[9] staff had children themselves.' Paul remembers, 'I just simply took myself over to the baby and followed the baby through the whole process. Just silently, just there. People knew I was there [and I] went through the process, because some-one needed to carry the burden.'

Later Paul wondered if 'the presence of a chaplain somehow gave them fuller permission to do their job of science, knowing that someone else was doing the job of love and faith'.[10]

Week after week chaplains are *present* in cafeterias and wards, in offices and playgrounds, singing their God-song by exemplifying, as best they can, the love of Christ and the fruit of the Spirit.[11] As they build relationships, they get to know the constraints of those in leadership, the concerns of workers, people's longings for security and hopes for their children. They may also pray with people, aware that, even for those who profess no faith, a prayer offered sensitively in the context of a respectful relationship can bring comfort and hope. Their presence is a reminder of another set of values, another kingdom where compassion and justice rank ahead of market forces and bottom lines.

If we take a leaf out of the chaplains' book, we simply begin by 'being out there' – faithfully, frequently, strolling around the streets, sitting in the local café, shopping at the market, engaging deeply with the life we find around us, with the sole intention of building trust and making a connection with the people. We join Jesus in 'listening' to the environment in which people live, the systems that affect them, the people who hold power over them, and the cultural traditions and practices that influence decision-making and freedom of speech. We learn more about what the

9 Disaster Victim Identification staff.

10 Melissa Parsons, *From Rubble to Resurrection: Churches Respond in the Canterbury Quakes*, Daystar Books, Auckland, NZ, 2014, pp. 117–18.

11 Galatians 5.22: love, joy, peace and so on.

people value, how they celebrate and mourn, what they delight in and what they find hard about living in this particular part of the world. In doing so, *we become honorary chaplains to our neighbourhood.*

Hospitality

When we consider how often a meal was the setting for significant encounters in the stories of Jesus,[12] it's not surprising that the sharing of food in a safe space often contributes to the emergence of *communitas*. I've seen this dynamic at work in Taranaki Cathedral's Community Café, set up following conversations with community groups seeking a warm and welcoming environment for those on the margins.[13] Over time, those who came, initially to eat the freshly cooked crêpes, have begun to help in the kitchen or wait on the tables. Single parents call in with their children before school; those who are lonely or have mental health issues sit with parishioners or folk from the wider community and talk over toast and porridge. Much food is donated, all proceeds go to responsible aid agencies, and *communitas* is happening.

It's challenging enough to broaden our perspective as a church and actively move into the community. It can be another challenge to notice what God is already doing through other groups of people trying to live out the gospel, whether or not they would specifically name that as their motivation. Simply charting the locations of church, temple, synagogue or mosque in our area is a start. Respectful connections with other faith groups can be made through a gathering of local leaders or through our natural networks. Perhaps we can explore offering hospitality on special feast days; perhaps we will be invited to weddings conducted in another tradition. Such relationships will build co-operation and bear witness to the wider community that it is possible for

---

12 See e.g. Luke 7, the Pharisee's dinner invitation; Mark 14.12–26, the Last Supper; Luke 14.12–14, whom to invite; John 21.1–12, post-resurrection breakfast on the beach.

13 If people can afford to, they pay 50p per item. Some donate much more. See www.taranakicathedral.org.nz/community-cafe.php.

'religious' people to work together for everyone's benefit. From there may come opportunities for deeper dialogue, collaboration on community projects, the chance to contribute to public worship at special events, or to begin exploring interfaith prayer.

⌘

People are responding to God's invitation to move beyond their churches to partner God in bringing abundant life to others. If we are well formed in our own faith and well supported by a loving church community, we can risk the inevitable uncertainty of venturing into the sort of territory described in the above examples. If we trust the Holy Spirit, we do not need to know how the venture will turn out, we have only to be listening for our 'orders of the day' – the *one next step* that God provides for us.

That is our faith. Let us not hinder God.[14]

⌘

Going Deeper: Listening to Our Communities

- Setting aside your church participation for now, recall a time when you joined a new community – such as an interest group, service or sporting club or a hobby class. What helped or hindered your sense of belonging? As far as you can deduce, would you describe this group as community or *communitas*?

- How well do you know other local Christian ministers? What is your experience of other religious groups within your neighbourhood? How might increased co-operation develop? Talk to God about anything that concerns you.

14 Acts 11.17.

Imagine the route you would take if you were walking around your neighbourhood for an hour. Ask the Holy Spirit to help you make a list of things that concern or frighten you, as well as the things that interest or even excite you. Spend some time taking each item to prayer, inviting God to be with you.

Go for a walk around your neighbourhood, paying attention to the things you identified above. Then take time to listen to the sounds around you: from nature; machinery, aircraft, trains or traffic; silence; human interaction: laughter, arguing, children or the elderly; different languages.
What might it be like to live in this environment?

☺☺ Meet with your PowerPod partners and compare your answers to the above questions. Notice any common themes or sense of being drawn to a particular area, situation or group of people. Then bring your discoveries to God and spend time in contemplative prayer, waiting on God in the silence to discern your 'next step'.

What constitutes 'spiritual conversation'?

When I think about public expressions of the Christian faith my mind flicks to adolescent memories of street-corner evangelists, and the feelings of resistance their rhetoric provoked in me. Instead of being drawn closer to the God of mercy, justice and love I've since come to know in Jesus, I was pushed further away, unwilling to risk engaging in conversation for fear of being overwhelmed by their intensity.

This was in the days when Christianity was still a familiar part of the dominant culture, particularly in the UK; well before we entered the 'post-Christendom' era. Now when we're in conversation, we can no longer assume a common understanding of, or respect for, the teachings of Jesus and the institution of the Church, fractured as it is by time-consuming arguments over sexuality, at the expense of focusing our attention on intentional formation in discipleship and witness.

So as we venture beyond our church setting, we cannot go with the expectation of shared experience or knowledge; instead we are called to go in respectful humility, as open-hearted and Jesus-minded disciples, following him into a new environment.

We will find that some people in this new environment do still have some connection with 'religion', but there are increasing numbers who don't. For example, data from the British Social Attitudes Survey (BSAS) shows that over the period 1983 to 2014:

- The Church of England population has nearly halved (from 16.5m to 8.6m).
- The Catholic population has remained relatively steady (from 4.1m to 4m).

- o Non-Christian religious numbers have increased fivefold (from 0.8m to 4m).
- o Persons of no religious affiliation have nearly doubled (from 12.8m to 24.7m).[1]

Those who ticked the 'no religious affiliation' box may belong to two quite different groups:

- The ***spiritual but not religious***, who may still have a belief in 'something other' or an awareness of the sacred dimension of life. However, instead of this being expressed through institutionalized religion, they may fashion individual mosaics of spirituality in which some aspects of the great faith traditions of the world sit alongside values and practices from humanist, esoteric, indigenous or pagan viewpoints. Such a personal spirituality attempts to address fundamental issues of meaning and purpose, inner transformation, growing affinity with others, concern for the earth and connection with the sacred. However, the 'I–Thou' of classic Christian engagement with the personal, loving mystery of God may be missing; the gospel imperative to serve others may be replaced by serving self.
- The ***churchless Christians***, who have, usually after many years, made the decision to cut ties with the institutional Church. Helen Ebaugh,[2] a former nun who researched the process of leaving important commitments, identified four stages of this difficult journey:
  - o Doubt, often triggered by personal events or dissatisfaction with the church leadership or structures.
  - o Seeking and weighing alternatives.
  - o Negotiating turning points.
  - o Developing a new sense of identity.

Those who have left inward-facing church congregations may have done so seeking a more practical and to them more authentic expression of faith in action. God remains at the centre of their

---

1 http://faithsurvey.co.uk/blog/religion-in-the-uk-1983-2014.

2 H. R. F. Ebaugh, *Becoming an EX: The Process of Role Exit*, University of Chicago Press, Chicago, 1988.

lives; they meet as smaller groups of like-minded believers, committed to the way of Jesus and building community

As well as the 'spiritual but not religious' and the 'churchless Christians', the diverse landscape beyond the church will also include:

- People of different ethnicities and faiths – some well established in our neighbourhood, others newly arrived following long journeys with trauma and sadness as travelling companions; some deeply religious and wedded to their cultures, others wanting to leave behind what they perceive as constricting expectations associated with particular religions or cultural groups.
- Passionate workers for justice, social equality and the care of creation – the very things we as church identify as gospel imperatives, but too often fail to address at a congregational level.
- Those who are apathetic about anything to do with matters of faith, who see God, religion, the Church and the spiritual life as irrelevant as they struggle to find shelter, food, work, belonging.
- People who are grappling with 'spooky' experiences or caught up in spiritual activities that have begun to frighten them or disconnect them from their friends or family.
- Those who, in the grip of an addiction, seek support not condemnation, and have had to go outside the Church to find it.
- Those who are linked to the LGBTQ community, whose experience of Christianity may be of bullying and vitriol rather than welcome and compassion.
- Vocal atheists who are keen to engage in intellectual arguments about matters of faith.

🕯 Consider the list above and how it relates to the people you know in your neighbourhood or networks.
For whom do you feel a natural empathy? Which people alarm you? Talk to God about both.
☺☺ Compare your answers with others in your small group or PowerPod.

⌘

We can't expect to go into this diverse spiritual environment with carefully prepared responses to every situation. Instead we go in humility with the Holy Spirit as our teacher, trusting that if we do our part to keep our connection with God alive and are prepared to be open about where God has met us in our own experience, we will be given what we need to say, when we need it.[3] This story illustrates that principle:

> Years ago at the age of 40 I had a miscarriage. After I got back from hospital I remember feeling so, so sad that this last chance for a second baby had gone. But as I sat there, what came to me was the desire to name this child and commend her to God. There were tears but there was also a sense of anchoring her in the reality of God's love and our family life. I think of Sarah Elizabeth often, especially on her due date each year.
>
> A couple of weeks after the miscarriage, when I was back on deck and doing my chaplaincy round at the power station, I came upon a staff member who had miscarried six months earlier. When she had told me her story I briefly mentioned my recent experience and shared what I had found helpful. 'Can you really do that – even though it was only a tiny scrap?' she asked haltingly. I nodded. 'Every life matters to God.' There was a thoughtful silence before we talked about options.[4] She decided she would approach her partner and other children to see if they would like to name and commend the little one to God together, using a little ritual of their own making. When I saw her a couple of weeks later, she met me in peace, and shared the story of their child's farewell.

I had not expected that particular conversation; nor had I anticipated that such recent experience would be used for someone else's comfort. I was reminded again of the pattern of consoling others with the consolation we have ourselves received. That's

3 Jesus encouraged his disciples to trust this dynamic, even if they were brought to court and needed to defend their decision to follow Jesus (see Luke 12.11–12).

4 For example, naming and commending the baby right then; meeting her later in the day to talk further; coming to church to have a little service in the chapel; putting together a little service for me to lead or them to use at home; making their own ritual.

how God seems to do things – even our hard times can lead to God's grace and personal care being shared with others.

Each one of you reading this book has extensive life experience. You will have negotiated major human transitions, some planned and some sudden or shocking. You will have seen people at their best and at their worst and been in both places yourself. Like the toy horse in *The Velveteen Rabbit*, you may bear the marks of being 'real' – showing signs of wear and tear, no longer so concerned about other people's expectations or your own, content simply to be yourself as an adult child of God, open to the ongoing wisdom of the Holy Spirit, being Christ's hands and voice among those you meet.

This reflection question encourages you to connect with stories whose essence you might be willing to share with those you meet as you wander the neighbourhood, so it's worth sitting down with a coffee or your favourite tea, allowing yourself a good chunk of uninterrupted time.

Write down some of your key life experiences, and then ask yourself:

- How did this experience affect me?
- What questions did this experience raise in me?
- How aware was I of God before/during/after that experience?
- What did I learn about myself, about others, about the wider community, about God?
- How has this experience already shaped my ministry/been shared with others?
- Which Jesus-story is relevant to this experience?

⌘

Early in our spiritual journey it's often easier to notice God's hand at work in retrospect as we recognize how different events have deepened our trust, diverted us from our God-path or brought us back to the Way. However, once we begin regular theological reflection, become aware of God in the ordinariness of life and have a routine of spiritual practices including listening prayer,

God's activity in our lives is recognized more clearly. We notice where grace strengthens or consoles us, where love challenges us and where God is with us in the midst of trials and setbacks. We become present to what God is doing in real time – *right now*.

This growing God-awareness helps us to connect with the people we meet and to trust God to be with us as conversations unfold. Within the context of our congregations, among 'churchless Christians' or spiritual seekers in the community, people may welcome the chance to talk through significant issues such as:

- vocation
- life's meaning and purpose
- suffering
- prayer
- apologetics – making a rational defence of the faith, not apologizing for it
- ways of being church – what prompts thanksgiving or provokes consternation.

And because God's loving embrace includes *all* people and the *whole* of life, then *any* conversation that opens up the 'deep-down things' of a person's life can be considered 'spiritual':

- ethical dilemmas in the workplace
- personal well-being or unease, belonging or isolation, illness or accident, the impact of addiction
- finding a partner, raising children, caring for the elderly, domestic violence, family relationships
- making big decisions
- housing, work, environmental or social justice issues
- abuse in all its forms
- wonder and beauty, imagination and innovation
- life transitions, endings and beginnings, grief and loss
- scientific discoveries and inventions made for hope and healing rather than selfish gain
- fear of the future or a sense of powerlessness in the face of global upheaval.

🕯 What is your experience of significant conversations on any of the topics named above?
How did your own experience of grace/God's provision help you to listen well and offer support?

Holding a sacred space in which people can *safely* talk about *whatever matters* to them is the first step in spiritual conversation. For many people, at the core of their stories will be the tension between fear and love: the voice of fear is strident and attention-grabbing and it is tempting to put a lot of energy into trying to help them overcome that fear. But as followers of Jesus, we know that the 'still, small voice of love' is always present. Spiritual conversations go deeper as we start to explore how God/loving presence[5] might be working in the lives of those we meet. God/Love questions emerge naturally as we get closer to people and they begin to trust us enough to speak about their deeper reality:

Love	Whom do you love? Who loves you?
Losses	What was it like when you had to leave ... (e.g. country/job/sick relative/course of study)? What/who helped you cope when ...? Where was God?
Church	Are/were you part of a faith community now/in the past? What made you stop going to church? How do you keep your God-connection alive now?
God-connection	When do you feel close to God? When do you feel further away from God? What do you think God is like? What way of seeing God helps you/puts you off?

5 1 John 4.7–8: 'Beloved, let us love one another, because love is from God; everyone who loves is born of God and knows God. Whoever does not love does not know God, for God is love.'

Forgiveness	What part has forgiveness played in your life? Whom have you wronged? Whom do you find it hard to forgive?
Community-connection	What sort of groups or community activities do you belong to? What do you get out of/contribute to being part of such a group?
Prayer	How has prayer been part of your life in the past? How about now? How does illness/pain/busyness affect your prayer? Who has prayed for you in the past? Who prays for you now?

🕯 What is your experience of asking or being asked these sorts of focused 'God/Love questions'?
How would different contexts affect your willingness to use questions like these?

⌘

Challenging spiritual conversations

A few pages ago I raised the issue of difficult spiritual conversations and the likelihood that we would encounter people who may want to talk about their struggles, disappointment with the Church or anger with God. I encouraged you to spend time looking seriously at your own experience and position in relation to those challenges. I've done the same over the years; below I've reflected on some areas that are often raised by people outside the church setting.

Homosexuality

I have to begin with the story of Mark:[6]

> Some years ago a tour of AIDS quilts[7] came to our town and was displayed in our church hall. Many went along out of curiosity, but I went to see whether there was a quilt for Mark. And there was.
>
> I was a naïve 20 year old when I had fallen in love with him at university, putting his lack of affection down to shyness. At the final end-of-year ball he told me he was gay. I was devastated – for him and for me. Though I wanted to be able to support him, I couldn't – I was young and conflicted by a depressing mixture of love and disgust, fearing for him because he was so vulnerable, questioning my femininity.
>
> University ended. We drifted apart and never saw each other again.
>
> I always wondered if he had found someone to love him, someone whom he could love.
>
> The quilt showed me that he had. And I was thankful.

Since then, in pastoral counselling or chaplaincy contexts, I've heard others' stories: gay students wrestling with thoughts of suicide, distraught after relationship breakdowns, or expressing their sexuality in risky behaviour; gay couples in settled monogamous relationships, contributing to their communities but wary of church participation; parents with adult gay children, anxious that no one (especially at church) should know, longing for their children to be content, worried about gay-bashing and grieving for grandchildren unborn.

Some of us will be in congregations that open their hearts to *all* people irrespective of gender, sexual orientation, race, ethnicity or any other factor that could be used to set up an 'us/them' division. However, the public perception of the Church's attitude towards issues around homosexuality[8] is largely shaped by media reports

6 Not his real name.

7 www.aidsquilt.org/about/the-aids-memorial-quilt.

8 For example, blessing of same-sex unions, the ordination of gay clergy and so on.

of the Church struggling to find a just way forward, as well as images of placard-waving 'Christians' proclaiming God's wrath and promising eternal damnation to LGBTQ people.

Gifted biblical scholars examining the few relevant biblical texts have argued persuasively for inclusion in, *and* exclusion from, the body of Christ. All I know is that Jesus said nothing about homosexuality and plenty about the poor, the widow and the orphan. 'Outsiders' of any persuasion were *welcomed* to his table. From my perspective, the Church can do no less.

Moral lapses or abuse by those who represent the Church

The power inherent in the position of a minister needs to be exercised with self-control and compassion but, sadly, there are examples of power misused, of self-indulgence or abuse masquerading as pastoral care. Some church hierarchies have colluded to protect the Church's image; thankfully, among church leaders now there is a commitment to transparency, to redressing of past wrongs and ensuring safe ministry practice. However, the pain of ministers' abuse of power lingers and we may still encounter criticism about church leadership, clergy failings and congregational hypocrisy. How do we respond?

As 'holy listeners' we listen as people tell their stories without trying to excuse the inexcusable. We listen to their pain or rage with compassion and patience, and express our genuine sorrow that they have experienced the opposite of what Jesus represents – freedom, life and peace and joy. And we offer them support as they consider options: further conversation, even confronting the offender and/or the institution.

Healing can take years as people work through the impact of what has been done to them by those claiming to represent God. Redeeming their internalized toxic image of God is not easy, but grace abounds. It is only when the person is well on the road to establishing a sense of their own worth and goodness, that they dare enter the latter stages of the healing journey and face the searing question: 'Where was God when ...?'

The 'Where is God?' question and suffering

Whether clergy or laity, in some way we are all affected by personal trauma, terrorist acts, disasters, political uncertainty, the desperation of refugee or trafficked humanity, and senseless conflict inflicting havoc on the innocent. When we wonder where God is in it all, it's crucial that, rather than turning our back on God in disgust, we tell God what's going on for us. Shaking our fist at God keeps alive our relationship with God – however strained – so communication can continue and we can remain open to God's revelation.

God gives us the freedom to make our own decisions and bear the consequences. This freedom, the natural laws of the earth and the reality of selfishness, greed and evil at work in systems, societies and individuals all contribute to tragedies and pain. And there is mystery and there is prayer – both of which play more of a part in the unfolding of events than we can begin to imagine.

Where I've got to in my thinking about the 'Where is God?' question is this: the God revealed to us both in the person of Jesus and the relational dance[9] of the Trinity is not a tyrannical taskmaster or faceless judge but a loving presence with us, in and through tragedy and pain. Some might still imagine God as distant and disinterested, but nothing could be further from the truth revealed in Jesus. As Bishop John Pritchard puts it:

> if we see God's interaction with his world not from above, from outside, but from beneath, from within the created order, then we have a very different image of God. This is a God who's limited himself to working *within* the system he's created. In the very act of creating he deliberately chooses to limit his absolute power in the interests of love.[10]

This deliberate choice gives Christianity its unique relevance: God is among us, working in and through us, enabling us to endure and transcend circumstances and suffering. Fired by the Spirit's

9 Perichoresis – see Jonathan Colman at https://musicanddancing.wordpress.com/perichoresis.

10 John Pritchard, *How to Explain Your Faith*, SPCK, London, 2006, pp. 67–8.

power and the example of Jesus, who suffered as a human being *and* as God, this choice helps us see the depth and breadth of the loving nature of a God who is prepared to be vulnerable in order to transform us from within.

The Church has been trying to get this 'God is with us' message out there since the beginning of Christianity. For example, in this sixteenth-century plague-hospital chapel painting by Matthias Grünewald,[11] Jesus is confrontingly portrayed as both crucified *and* afflicted with plague-type sores. While its grotesque detail may have been hard to bear for the plague-patients who gazed upon it, the presence of the sores on Jesus' body would have brought them an awareness that their Lord *was with them in their suffering*, that he not only understood it, but experienced it, as they did.

However, rather than offering the comradeship of Jesus on the cross to the whole of humanity, it's as if the institutional Church over time has allowed its core message of a generous Emmanuel to be diverted into a cul-de-sac of man-made legalism and arguments about who is in and who is out.

11 Mathias Grünewald, *Crucifixion*, from the Isenheim altarpiece in the Musée Unterlinden in Colmar.

That's where the challenging conversation may begin, but it doesn't have to end there. Each time 'bad things happen to good people', there is an opportunity to witness to God's presence in the midst of suffering and tragedy; to help people spot our God who is with people in the fear and panic, the blood and the pain, the facing of death, last thoughts of loved ones, the letting go of life. And rather than being overwhelmed by media images of tragedy, we can teach our children to look for God too in the selflessness of those who put themselves at risk; in the countless acts of kindness that flow into the affected communities and in the resolve that strengthens the human spirit in the face of threat.

Christians and the environment

Judging by the attendees at a recent global conservation project conference, most people who are trying to stem habitat loss and species extinction come from outside the church. If we venture into the field of environmental conservation we may well encounter some of the attitudes to Christianity that Peter Harris, founder of A Rocha, has been hearing for decades. This is what he had to say following the World Conservation Congress in September 2016:

> It does seem to our colleagues and friends in the conservation world that very few Christians care, even though they hear us say that we believe the earth is the Lord's, not merely an environment of 'natural resources' for human economic development. Conservationists hear messages of indifference, or worse, from some of the more vocal Christian leaders they encounter in the media. The prosperity gospel that resounds in so many parts of the world, with its unthinking embrace of unbridled consumption, makes no sense to those with an acute sense of limits and planetary boundaries. So many conservation leaders are not surprisingly sceptical that the Christian faith is transformative.
>
> Until recently, the conservation movement has been overwhelmingly secular. But the sense here is that this is a moral and even a spiritual crisis. As Gus Speth, who helped found the Natural Resources Defense Council and was dean of the Yale

School of Forestry and Environmental Studies, told a British radio presenter in 2013:

> I used to think that top global environmental problems were biodiversity loss, ecosystem collapse, and climate change. I thought that with 30 years of good science we could address these problems, but I was wrong. The top environmental problems are selfishness, greed, and apathy, and to deal with these we need a spiritual and cultural transformation. And we scientists don't know how to do that.[12]

We need spiritual and cultural transformation – not just the testing of more hypotheses or spending billions on complex research, but growing participation in practices that address both the spiritual poverty of our time and the transformation of our culture into one that addresses human need and is committed to equitable distribution of resources and protection of the environment.

Humans are created for relationship with God. There is an often unnamed longing for the 'more' that is not man-made but God-breathed. We can help transform this longing into relationship if we are actively singing our God-songs in the community, engaging in spiritual conversation and seeking to be involved in making our neighbourhood a life-giving place for all its inhabitants.

⌘

Going Deeper: What Constitutes 'Spiritual Conversation'?

Recall any recent spiritual conversations you've had. Remember as best you can the content, the emotions and thoughts expressed by the other person and your own emotions and thoughts.

What was your assessment of how it went? What might you do differently?

12 Peter Harris, founder of A Rocha, 'A Report from the World Conservation Congress, 1–10 September 2016'. First published on *Christianity Today*, 8 September 2016. See http://blog.arocha.org/en/why-conservation-is-a-gospel-issue.

☺☺ In your small group or with your PowerPod partner/s, review the list of God/Love questions.
Try some out on each other, perhaps role-playing how the conversation might unfold.
What questions do you struggle with and why?
What questions might you want to add to the list?

What is your experience of walking alongside those on the margins because of homosexuality and/or
those who've been badly hurt by 'the Church' in some way?
What temptations have you faced in your ministry to date?
How have you found a way through them?

What has most challenged your faith? Who has helped you/ is supporting you?

Try these conversation starters on your friends:

- How might we become more involved in working for the healing of creation in our local area?
- What might the church look like at its best?
- How might God want to meet you today?
- If you could tell our church what you'd like to see changed about the way we do things, what would you say?

Sharing our own stories

> My mouth will tell of your righteous acts,
> of your deeds of salvation all day long,
> though their number is past my knowledge.
>
> *Psalm 71.15*

We often tip-toe into personal storytelling, gauging the risk of going deeper, wondering whether people will laugh, turn away, gossip or think less of us. It is only with someone we really trust, or whose timely presence provides a much-needed chance to be heard, that a story from a protected part of our experience might be brought to the surface. That's where soul connection is made – when someone has the chance to tell a potent, personal story to a sensitive, compassionate listener. It's that quality of connection that we want to offer in the neighbourhood as we follow where Jesus leads. However, although it's reasonable to expect that soul connection to be embodied in our church culture, sadly, unless we're part of a small group or we meet others socially outside church, we can go to church services for years and still not know the stories of those whom we sit beside, week in and week out. But it doesn't have to be that way.

In 2015 an Auckland church released a remarkable book. Simply titled *St Paul's Stories*, it contains 128 stories from parishioners who responded to an invitation from their vicar to share a story that would illustrate what is was like to experience God's reality in everyday life. As Jonny Grant (vicar) and Esther Grant (managing editor) write in the Foreword:

> The stories contained in these pages provide glimpses of God, big and small. They have taken courage to write. They are not

> carefully crafted profiles but honest accounts of real life. They are a precious gift ...
>
> It is only when we experience God's love that we are able to love Him. And it is only when we get to know each other that we can step into the journey of loving each other well.
>
> We hope that in these pages you will encounter Jesus, and that you might be inspired to ask those around you, *What's your story?* And when the same is asked of you, may you have the courage to answer![1]

The St Paul's stories include those of primary school-age children telling of how God answered their prayers about lost pets, broken friendships and family illness; God meeting adolescents and young people in their doubts and searching; people being supported through family disruption, redundancy, serious health issues.

The whole book is full of people singing their God-songs and giving witness to the reality of a loving, healing, forgiving, faithful God.

What is your response to the St Pauls' initiative?
How might 'only when we get to know each other can we step into the journey of loving each other well' unfold in your faith context?

⌘

Mostly our God-stories will tell of events and life transitions that fall within the experience of most of us – births, deaths, family ups and downs, friendships, moving house, finding work, making a life for ourselves – the everyday weaving of threads familiar to many people. These 'ordinary' stories have immense value as testimony when we notice and name the God-colour – the thread of grace which, though invisible to many, holds people together, as my good friend Eirene writes:

1 Esther Grant (Managing Editor), *St Paul's Stories*, St Paul's Anglican Church, Symonds Street, Auckland, NZ, 2015, p. 5.

When my husband's health deteriorated and he developed signs of early dementia, I thought it best for us to relocate from New Plymouth to Auckland to be closer to our three daughters. I was thinking ahead, trying to make life easier for all of us so they would not have a long drive if things got bad for us and we needed their immediate presence and help. I also thought that I could be of assistance to them and their families when they needed it, and also longed to see more of my sister.

Before his illness my husband had managed our finances, did the weekly shopping and cooked our evening meals with skill and ease while I was working. However, within a few months that confident being had disappeared, and another emerged who had lost the ability to make decisions and manage all of these tasks. So I learned how to sort finances and years of paperwork, disposed of a whole workshop of tools and much household furniture, and found the best land agent who cared for us honestly during the selling process.

Those last months in NP flew past, and I sold or gave away everything I could, feeling pleased with my new acumen. I accumulated a stash of cash from the sales of goods which was immensely helpful in the weeks to come. My husband had an emergency operation three weeks before we left which was a huge shock to all of us, and he was very fragile. The night before we left, I was blessed with some lovely friends who came to help with a big house-clean after the large furniture was loaded on the truck. That night I read my map and made copious notes. The next day we were to drive the 250 miles to Auckland on some beautiful but challenging roads.

As soon as I woke that morning I prayed and prayed for safety on the road, for guidance to stop when I was weary as I had not done many long distance trips before this, and for the knowledge to help in our new life ahead. I felt an immense calmness, no anxiety, and a pure optimism for our future. I felt enfolded in God's arms as I drove, with my very ill husband propped up beside me, and I just knew we would be cared for. And it happened.

> Now we have been here almost two years in our little house, surrounded by others our age, and I feel secure in the knowledge that I did the right thing. Three weeks after we arrived here my husband had another serious operation, and for months afterwards he sat cuddled up among blankets on our couch, and our life moved onwards. He did not know where we were, what had happened to him or why we had left our familiar surroundings. But he was enfolded in love and care, and these days he is relaxed and secure in our new life, although he still does not know our address! We see our families often, and share our lives with them and with my sister. How lucky we are.
>
> As the hymn says, 'All I have needed Thy hand has provided', and these words are in my mind every day.

I share this in detail because it is in the detail that God appears – *all* that Eirene and her husband needed, God provided. Her story might take a few minutes to tell but imagine what it reveals to someone about God's faithfulness and about Eirene's capacity to share her needs with God, and rejoice in God's provision.

🕯 Do you have stories like this in your own life – or in the lives of those you know? Have they been shared?

⌘

It's a delight to share stories of God's grace with others and to know that by doing so, we are witnessing to God's care and presence with us in the whole of life. And it's comparatively easy to tell stories about our successes and achievement as the world judges these things, or about our participation in activities that gain the approval of our listeners. But stories that emerge from the darker depths of our human experience are another thing altogether. We think twice about revealing stories that speak of shame, identity, failure, guilt or tragic loss:

- ***Shame***[2] – strikes at the core of who we are and leaves us feeling there is something fundamentally wrong with us – sadly it is a common legacy of abuse, especially sexual abuse. Worryingly, compulsive use of pornography is accelerating in Western society; Christians are not immune to its seduction and often hide their addiction because of the shame they feel.
- ***Identity*** – affects our sense of belonging and connection to a wider group – tensions around adoption, secrets about paternity, never being taught our cultural practices all cut deeply
- ***Failure*** – unpleasant though it is, failure helps us face our limitations and gives us an opportunity to learn from our mistakes and deepen our humility. We all fail, we all fall, we are all still loved by God.
- ***Guilt*** – brings our actions into the spotlight – things we've done that are wrong, stupid, hurtful to others. We resist revealing a side to ourselves that shows we are not perfect.
- ***Tragic loss*** – when someone we love dies in horrible circumstances, finding competent support to address both the grief and the post-traumatic stress can be problematic; it's also hard to find ways of expressing our very natural anger, particularly if that anger is directed towards God.

Spend some time reflecting on how the five areas listed above relate to your personal stories.

What is your experience of sharing such stories with God; with other people?

If painful memories come to the surface, maybe even with tears, seek out someone with whom you can safely share your story. The healing process may be hard and slow, but what God does in you as you face these memories will ultimately enable you to be there for others with profound empathy. We console others with the consolation we have ourselves received from God (2 Corinthians 1.3–4).

---

2 For more information on the distinction between 'shame' and 'guilt', see James M. Bowler, 'Shame: A Primary Root of Resistance to Movement in Spiritual Development', in *Presence: An International Journal of Spiritual Direction* 3:3, September 1997.

However far 'down' we may think we have gone; however shadowed our interior landscape, we know that Jesus meets us there by his Spirit and can lift us 'out of the miry bog, and set [our] feet upon a rock' (Psalm 40.2b).

What I've seen repeatedly in spiritual direction and retreat ministry is that God steadfastly offers us healing even if we have, like the woman in Luke 13.10–17, been 'bent over' with inner pain for decades.

> Some years ago at a retreat, a woman spoke for the first time about an abortion she'd had in traumatic circumstances. For over 60 years she had carried the shame, guilt and grief of what had happened; as she aged the emotional pain seemed to be getting worse. I listened to her story, to her remorse and regret.
>
> With tears we turned to the rite of repentance and absolution, and named her baby before God.
>
> Our faithful God met her in her pain; she was 'raised up'.
>
> That is good news; that is transformation.

⌘

On a lighter note: as with most things, singing our God-song will come more naturally if we've had the opportunity to practise! This can happen formally or informally, but the more we do it, the easier it becomes. Just as teenage would-be singing sensations start in their bedrooms, we might begin by telling our God-story to ourselves, exploring in our journal classic spiritual direction questions such as: 'What's God been up to in my life lately?' or 'Where have I noticed signs of grace, or light in the darkness?'

We might go on to describe a special God-moment to a trusted friend or sympathetic family member. If it's part of our church practice, we may be able to share our God-story as part of a testimony, magazine, panel or interview slot within a regular service. And if our church is using this book to help form witnesses, you can practise in your PowerPod!

When it's time to venture into the community, prepare with prayer, and be open to the Spirit. Remember that *you do not have to make anything happen.* Take to heart these words from the ordination liturgy:

> Serve patiently and cheerfully,
> remembering that the work you are called to do is God's work;
> it is in God's hand, and it is done in God's name to God's glory.
> Follow Christ whose servant you are.[3]

⌘

An important shift happens when we 'go public'. No longer is an example of God's grace confined to our own experience; instead it is set free to continue its work among those who hear it proclaimed. Of course such proclamation needs prayerful preparation, but it also requires an honest look at our motivation to ensure we're not being big-headed or trying to make a point at someone else's expense and, most importantly, that our focus is on how God has met us in our dilemma *and* can meet others. So that's what I had in mind as I prepared to preach one Sunday.

For years I had been too ashamed to let others at church know about my chronic anxiety and episodes of depression. I thought people would that think if I were a 'better Christian' I should 'rise above' such things, that I 'ought' to be able to get rid of this 'thorn in my flesh' (2 Corinthians 12.7) by will power and prayer, but it persisted. And when my Bishop suggested I apply to do a course at St George's College in Jerusalem, the idea of *flying* from New Zealand to the Middle East *alone* sent my anxiety into overdrive.

Years ago I'd been taught to keep my own experience out of my preaching, but now I realize the value of the occasional personal story to illustrate how God can work in a person's life, so this is what I shared:

> Two weeks before I was due to leave NZ, a woman who'd recently flown to Israel via London 'happened' to visit our church and told me all about the airport security checks she'd experienced. Freaking out inwardly, I went home and poured

3 *A New Zealand Prayer Book*, Collins, Auckland, NZ, p. 906.

out to my husband and then to Jesus my fear of being taken aside or searched or interrogated. As I prayed, slowly something in my thinking changed: instead of feeling afraid, I realized that this might give me a chance to talk about the reason for my trip – getting to know Jesus better.

At Heathrow the check-in for El Al airlines was in a corner of the terminal – so if a bomb went off the damage would be contained, I thought! There were sniffer dogs and armed police stationed all around. A very serious young man with a clipboard asked me what seemed endless questions about my intentions. Jesus' name popped up often in my replies. Then my suitcase went through the machine and, sure enough, I was pulled aside so they could investigate the long cylindrical object the X-ray had picked up. Behind the screen, as a humourless woman looked through the contents of my suitcase, I talked about where I was going and why, and again Jesus' name popped up quite often! Finally the official held up the offending object and a slight smile emerged when I told her it was a large jar of Marmite for a friend who was then chaplain at St George's College in Jerusalem.

As I walked through the passenger security checks before boarding, up on the wall was a billboard with the words GO CONFIDENTLY in metre-high letters! I've no idea what it was advertising but I'd recently discovered the building blocks of this word – *con* + *fidere* – literally meaning 'with faith' – not *my* faith but *faith in God*. And so, warmed by God's reassurance, I flew to Israel.

God totally transformed my anxiety about that journey and made it possible. Although I still get anxious from time to time, I know that Jesus bears this wound in my nature with me to this day. It has brought me closer to him, and I know that he will bear your wounds too if you choose to bring them to him.

It was clear that what I'd preached touched a chord with those in the congregation, some of whom were moved to tell me their own stories of anxiety or depression and/or God's provision for them in scary situations. I guess I became more real to them and more approachable. Being prepared to share something of our own God-stories with our congregation, if done sensitively, can help to shatter the false image of leaders always 'having it all together'.

🕯 What's your experience of sharing a personal story with others you lead or care for?
What has it been like for you to hear a leader speak honestly about a personal struggle? In the telling, did the story serve to give glory to God and remind listeners that God is with us whatever we face?

⌘

Let's finish this section with some words from Paul's letter to the Romans, 10.14–17 (*The Message*):

> But how can people call for help if they don't know who to trust? And how can they know who to trust if they haven't heard of the One who can be trusted? And how can they hear if nobody tells them? And how is anyone going to tell them, unless someone is sent to do it? That's why Scripture exclaims,
>
> A sight to take your breath away!
> Grand processions of people
> telling all the good things of God!
>
> But not everybody is ready for this, ready to see and hear and act. Isaiah asked what we all ask at one time or another: 'Does anyone care, God? Is anyone listening and believing a word of it?' The point is: Before you trust, you have to listen. But unless Christ's Word is preached, there's nothing to listen to.

We are the word Jesus preaches to our contemporaries.
Our song is the song Jesus sings in and through us.
He is Emmanuel – God with us.

Spiritual needs and a Christian response: sharing Jesus-stories

> Devote yourselves to prayer, keeping alert in it with thanksgiving ... [praying] ... that God will open to us a door for the word, that we may declare the mystery of Christ ... that I may reveal it clearly ...
>
> *Colossians 4.2–4*

Listening to others' stories and singing something of our God-song build bridges into communities beyond the institutional Church. But if we really want to offer people a Christian response to the spiritual needs they face, we need to be prepared to talk about Jesus, to be so familiar with his life that we can chat easily about him as we might about a dear friend. In the wider community, we usually hear the name of Jesus used only as an exclamation or worse. How is the name of Jesus going to re-enter the public arena in respectful and engaging dialogue unless we begin to challenge its gross misuse and are prepared to witness to what we know of Jesus?

If we make the Gospels our foundational reference for the Christian content of our spiritual conversations, we will find that in the Jesus-stories we see reflected the full range of human emotion and struggle, as well as a much-needed clarity about God's nature: caring for those on the margins and full of steadfast love, rather than hell-bent on our destruction.

We will be able to talk about Jesus as a real person who experienced common human suffering and struggles: betrayal, persecution, frustration, pettiness among his closest friends, the straitjacket of religious legalism, disappointment and deep grief, forgiveness and reconciliation, and the anguished anticipation of his own death and the leaving behind of those he loved.

We can also talk about Jesus' relationship with God – in nights of prayer, in times of revelation at baptism and transfiguration, in the mystery of miracles and healings, in deepening trust and obedience even to death, and in the wonder of resurrection and the gift of his ongoing friendship and guidance by his Spirit.

And so we come to the crux of spiritual conversations – the identification of and response to spiritual needs, which, *if fulfilled*, enable us to live true to our uniqueness as beings made in the image of God.[1] The only part of ourselves that can continue to develop as we age is our spiritual life, but spiritual growth can be compromised when faculties and focus may be failing. So if we can recognize and engage with spiritual needs *when we are younger*, when all being well we have better emotional and mental capacity, we can spend time building a relationship with God that will serve us well as we enter the latter years. This is what happened for a woman in her 90s:

> When Ruth very nearly died in the rest-home lounge, staff were quick to help her and she survived. She had always come to services and prayers so I knew her faith was strong and real. Later that day, when she had recovered from the shock of that life-threatening moment and family had visited, I sat down with her quietly and asked her if she'd like to talk about what had happened. She began with what I had already gleaned from other people's comments, but then she said, 'He was right there – even though it was very frightening – Jesus – he was right there.'

1 Nursing researchers Judith Shelly and Sharon Fish (*Spiritual Care: The Nurse's Role*, 3rd edn, Inter-Varsity Press, Downers Grove, IL, 1988) identified the need for forgiveness, the need for relationship and the need to find meaning and purpose in one's life. Other researchers have added to this list as more understanding is reached about the pivotal place of spiritual well-being at all stages of our lives, e.g. Elizabeth MacKinlay, *Spiritual Growth and Care in the Fourth Age of Life*, Jessica Kingsley Publishers, London, 2006, and Harold G. Koenig, *Spirituality in Patient Care*, 2nd edn, Templeton Foundation Press, London, 2007.

Ruth was blessed by her strong, long-standing relationship with Jesus, which enabled her to withstand the sternest test. But not everyone is like Ruth. It's one of the saddest things to see elderly people who have been exposed to Sunday School or active in the church for most of their lives, still *not really knowing* that God loves them and is with them. These people form a significant number of our current congregations and the duty of care we owe them goes far beyond keeping them comfortable with more of the familiar, until we take their funerals. We have a responsibility to offer them opportunities for spiritual growth,[2] a chance to have their spiritual needs met and above all, the comfort of knowing that God *is with them* all the way home.

🕯 As you read through the spiritual needs section below, consider which are currently being met in your life.
Which needs remain unmet? How might you pray about these? You may also want to reflect on how these resonate with someone whom you know well.

Each of the spiritual needs below, presented in no particular order, is followed by a personal question and encourages you to think of a story from your own life that relates to this need. Finally, for each need there is a Scripture story for reflection – chosen because it raises issues that are relevant in contemporary human experience and has something to say either about Jesus' humanity and divinity or the significant people in his life and their experience of loving and losing.

1 *A need for meaning and purpose*

Many of us find meaning and purpose in being 'useful', perhaps by doing something for others or being committed to a role, job or community to which we can make a contribution. However, should something affect our ability to be productive or participative, what has brought meaning and purpose in the past may no

2 You may like to check out my *Creative Ideas for Ministry with the Aged*, Canterbury Press, Norwich, 2014.

longer do so. For example, those of us who find a sense of meaning and identity primarily in our work may struggle when we stop work to raise a family, face redundancy or retirement. When our 'reason for being' dissolves into thin air, we become vulnerable, invisible.

- What gives your life meaning now?
  What story comes to mind about a time you struggled to find meaning or purpose?
  How did your faith/relationship with God/Jesus help you?
- *Read and reflect on Luke 2.41–51, the story of Jesus left behind and found in the temple.*

2 *A need for connection with other people, for significant relationships*

These days, people are extremely mobile for all sorts of reasons; distance can often separate family members; busyness can compromise contact and undermine bonds of friendship. Yet as the Trinity reveals, we are created to be in relationship.

- Who is important to you at this stage of your life?
  How satisfying is the contact you have with them?
  What story can you tell about a time when you felt disconnected, alone, isolated?
  How was Jesus/God present to you?
- *Read and reflect on Luke 10.38–42, the story of Jesus with Martha and Mary.*

3 *A need to grieve*

The complex emotional journey of grieving takes time, but 'grief work' may not be completed because circumstances and cultural expectations dictate that we have to 'get on with life'. However, if we experience grief upon grief, sooner or later we will reach a point where even a minor loss can trigger extreme dislocation and sadness. It is natural to want to avoid the pain of grieving, but if we are supported through the 'valley of the shadow', our compassion and resilience increase and we can be there for others in their time of need.

- How do you grieve when you lose someone or something you hold dear?
  How were you supported through a time of loss or grief? Where was God for you at the time? How did God's perceived presence or absence affect how you saw God then/see God now?
- *Read and reflect on John 11.17–37, the story of the death of Lazarus and Jesus' response.*

4 *A need for reconciliation and forgiveness*

Carrying grudges and denying our mistakes are contrary to what God longs for us. We are invited to put things right, to reconnect with estranged family or friends, to forgive ourselves for our failures and weakness.

- How does forgiveness figure in your life at the moment?
  What story comes to mind in which you were able to forgive or received forgiveness?
- *Read and reflect on John 21.9–17, the story of Jesus restoring the distraught Simon Peter to relationship.*

5 *A need to allow yourself to be cared for*

We come into this life needing to be nurtured; we often require a high level of care as ageing bites deeply. Yet in between we inhabit the lie of self-reliance and independence. So often we shut out other people's efforts to offer support because we think we should be able to manage on our own; by doing so, chances to build relationships of healthy interdependence are denied.

- How hard is it for you to let someone help you?
  What can you say about a time when you allowed someone to help you?

- *Read and reflect on Mark 14.3–9, the story of Jesus and the anointing at Bethany.*

6 A need for solitude and silence

Although those of us who are extraverted in temperament might think that the last thing we need is to be on our own with no one to talk to, it is surprising how beneficial time alone can be. A period of solitude can allow us the freedom to be ourselves, without having to pretend. Silence relieves us from the continual barrage of noise that twenty-first-century living imposes on urban dwellers. Into our quietening mind, the 'still, small voice' of God can whisper our name with love.

- How do you ensure you have some time for solitude and silence on a regular basis?
  What story comes to mind about a significant time of being on your own with God?
- *Read and reflect on Mark 1.35, the story of Jesus' own need for solitude and silence.*

7 A need to strengthen your connection with the divine/higher power/God

Recent science has suggested that human beings are 'hotwired for God'[3], and those of us who are Christian would agree that we are created in the image of God; that the divine Spirit dwells within us and is accessible through prayer and contemplation.

- What helps you connect with God/Jesus/higher power?
  What story comes to mind about a touch of God's grace or a spiritual experience?
- *Read and reflect on Mark 1.9–11, the story of Jesus' baptism.*

---

3 Andrew Newberg, Eugene D'Aquili and Vince Rause, *Why God Won't Go Away: Brain Science and the Biology of Belief*, Ballantine Books, New York, 2001.

8 A need to make sense of/transcend suffering

Suffering can overwhelm us if we lack skilled support and do not find a way of integrating our personal experience into a bigger story. The story of the passion of the human Jesus has extraordinary potency for those who are in the midst of suffering, for in his anguish they see their own. It is a natural step for us to speak of 'God with us' in Jesus, for Jesus understands the human experience and stands alongside us in solidarity, even as he absorbs the worst that humanity can do.

- What helps you cope with pain and suffering?
  What can you say about the link between the suffering of Jesus and your own suffering?
- *Read and reflect on Matthew 26.36–46, the story of Jesus in the garden of Gethsemane.*

9 A need to let go of control

Most of us struggle with control issues. It eases our anxiety to try to minimize the unknown and prepare for what we think lies ahead, but in reality of course, none of us knows what each minute will bring. The Christian spiritual journey is marked by opportunities for increasing levels of trust in the leading and merciful presence of God in whatever situations we encounter, and so we can expect God to place before us things that stretch us and push us further into the arms of Jesus.

- What is God inviting you to let go of at the moment?
  How have you experienced God's invitation to trust more deeply?
- *Read and reflect on Luke 23.39–46, the story of Jesus on the cross – the ultimate letting go.*

10 A need to prepare for death

Accident or terminal illness can strike at any age, and with it comes the work of facing our mortality or the death of a loved one. Ideally feelings can be expressed safely as they arise and there can be some movement towards a place of inner peace, but this does not happen unless we are helped to engage with the reality of what is happening and its implications.

Our responsibility as ministers is to initiate and enable the difficult conversations around suffering, dying and death with the seriously unwell, and their families.[4] *If* the connection to the Jesus- story is made, we can speak of 'Walking through the valley of the shadow of death' (Psalm 23), of Jesus knowing this path all too well[5] and having to face his own emotional anguish in the Garden of Gethesemane. We can offer the hope that the repentant thief knew when Jesus assured him: 'today you will be with me in Paradise' (Luke 23.43). We do not have to travel home to God on our own – Jesus is with us.

- Should you or a loved one have to face a terminal illness, what would you want to do?
  What story comes to mind of accompanying someone as they faced death?
- *Read and reflect on Mark 10.32–34, one of the accounts of Jesus predicting his death.*

11 *A need to review the way we see God*

Inevitably the way we saw God when we were younger will come to grief when faced with the doubts and disappointments of adulthood. But from the rubble of broken expectations and trauma, a new way of seeing God can emerge that has more to say about who God is in the ordinary mess and miracles of life.

- How would you describe the God you believe/don't believe in now?
  What would you say to someone about a time when you had to re-examine your image of God?
- *Read and reflect on Luke 13.34, the story of Jesus weeping over Jerusalem.*

---

4 Conversations about what might happen after death can emerge if they need to, with a focus on the mercy and love of God.

5 He travelled it once, and continues to travel it with those who die in awful circumstances, unattended or unloved.

12 *A need for hope*

In the midst of grief and loss, in the face of anxiety, there can still be hope.

- What enables you to maintain a hopeful outlook?
  What personal story illustrates the hope you have through your faith?
- *Read and reflect on Romans 8.38–39, rewriting it to reflect your own situation.*

The more we listen to people's stories, the more their spiritual needs will be revealed. The more willing we are to share relevant Jesus-stories, the more we can really start to offer something of what Jesus brings to people's lives: hope, peace, courage, strength, forgiveness, and companionship in whatever struggles they face. Speaking of Jesus naturally in this way enables us to name him as *the one who leads us* to Love, to God. Surely this is what lies at the core of John 14.6:

> Jesus said to him, 'I am the way, and the truth, and the life.
> No one comes to the Father except through me.'

In some parts of the Church, this verse is used as an argument against other religions or as a way of reinforcing people's need to make a personal commitment to Jesus in order to guarantee 'salvation', as if anything we did could make God love us more. But what if we were to see this verse as Jesus telling us to follow him because he best knows and reveals the fullness of God's nature as love, and longs for us to know that love for ourselves?

Andrew brought his brother Simon to meet Jesus (John 1.40–42).

Jesus wants to do the same for each one of us:

> 'Come and meet my dear dad. Get to know me and you'll get to know him and become a son or daughter just as I am. Be one with us and know the truth of being loved into fullness of life.'[6]

6 My paraphrase.

Standing up and speaking out

For everything there is a season ...
a time to keep silence, and a time to speak.
Ecclesiastes 3.1a, 7b

Those who believe that religion and politics aren't connected, don't understand either.
Mahatma Gandhi[1]

Being a kind and persistent Christian presence in the neighbourhood is a marvellous way to start building relationships and developing mutual trust. Sharing life stories and singing our God–song takes our commitment to the community to a new level. But that's not enough. As we open ourselves to loving those we've met, the more likely we are to become aware of unjust social structures,[2] and the more we'll be touched by the effects of political decisions on the vulnerable. And then we have a choice: do we stop at 'awareness', at unseen empathy, or do we allow prayer to move us into more visible action?

For some of us this step into the public arena will be daunting; for others a welcome chance to get our teeth into some positive action. Whatever our readiness to become the voice of Jesus speaking up for what is just and kind and hopeful, we can rely on the Spirit to give us the nudge, the words and the inner strength we need.

We can start small by writing letters to the newspaper, posting concerns on social media, signing online petitions. Those

1 Mahatma Gandhi. BrainyQuote.com, Xplore Inc, 2016. www.brainyquote.com/quotes/quotes/m/mahatmagan135298.html.

2 Anglican marks of mission. See 'Further reading'.

of us who express ourselves through the arts – music, painting, sculpture and so on – may offer works for an exhibition focused on themes relevant to faith or in conjunction with major festivals such as Easter, Pentecost or Christmas. We can attend public meetings and join or initiate action aimed at improving the situations that the local people or environment face. Righteous indignation coupled with committed prayer, creative protest, astute leadership and well-informed debate can overcome enormous odds.

Opportunities to 'stand up and speak out' will arise naturally; it's up to us to be willing to take them. For example:

- hosting a guest speaker from an aid agency or a social justice activist
- making a formal complaint to the media
- pointing out someone's abuse of the name of Jesus
- seeking election to a school board of governors or a charity's board of trustees
- supporting a colleague, injured by unsafe equipment at work, through a remediation process
- 'standing up and speaking out' when we see someone treated unfairly
- preparing and speaking to a submission about the proliferation of alcohol outlets
- going with a disempowered person to a court or custody hearing
- speaking out against domestic violence
- creating an art work with a justice focus
- chairing a meeting for a neighbourhood group about a local issue
- gathering a team to clean up blocked streams, replant river banks and beautify an urban area.

🕯/☺☺ Spend some time reviewing the list above – notice what you and your church community have already done, what appeals and what you pull back from. Talk to God about your discoveries and what you sense might be relevant in your context. Listen and allow the Spirit to soothe, guide or challenge you. Then talk about it with members of your PowerPod, before bringing it to those who can offer further discernment, resourcing, ongoing accountability and encouragement.

⌘

Earlier in this book we looked at the value of silence in deepening our relationship with God. We also acknowledged how listening/contemplative prayer can help us discern God's will for action. Inevitably, as we respond to God's call to serve our neighbourhood and communities, we will be called to stand up and speak out. The extent to which we can obey that call is a question for us to answer as individuals, but the impact of our witness can make all the difference. For example, without the effort of Russian grandmothers – 'babushkas' – who kept the Christian faith alive in spite of the systematic destruction and desecration of religious sites under Stalin, there would have been no resurgence of Christianity in Russia, nor the will to ensure the reconsecration of the fully rebuilt Cathedral Church of the Saviour in Moscow in 2000.[3]

History records the drastic consequences when people of faith fail to draw attention to movements that threaten human rights, freedom and justice. Martin Niemöller was a German Lutheran pastor and theologian born in Lippstadt, Germany, in 1892. An anti-communist, he initially supported Adolf Hitler, but became disillusioned when Hitler insisted on the supremacy of the state over religion. Niemöller led a group of German clergy opposed to Hitler, was arrested in 1937, and confined in Sachsenhausen and Dachau until his release by the Allies in 1945. After the Second World War, he continued in Germany as a clergyman and leading voice of penance and reconciliation for the German people. It was Niemöller who wrote:

> First they came for the Socialists, and I did not speak out – because I was not a Socialist.
> Then they came for the Trade Unionists, and I did not speak out – because I was not a Trade Unionist.

3 www.pattimaguirearmstrong.com/2012/08/russian-babushkas-rebuild-church.html.

> Then they came for the Jews, and I did not speak out – because I was not a Jew.
> Then they came for me – and there was no one left to speak for me.[4]

🕯 What parallels might be drawn between what Niemöller is saying and what we have been seeing on the world political stage over the last year? Socialists, Jews, trade unionists were the targets then – who are the targets in our generation?

Staying silent about injustice or speaking up for our faith involves choice – we know that sometimes that choice is literally between life and death, our own or those of people we love. Until faced with forced choices in times of war or horror, we don't know whether we'd collude with those in power, assert our agreement with dominant forces but seek ways to resist on the quiet, or whether we'd strongly stand up for what we know to be of enduring value, risking everything for Jesus.

There are countless martyrs in the history of the Church and more names added each year as a result of terrorism or violence. The martyred South American Archbishop Oscar Romero knew his life was at risk because he championed justice, but he continued to challenge not only the powers that enabled that injustice to continue, but also the Church:

> A church that doesn't provoke any crises, a gospel that doesn't unsettle, a word of God that doesn't get under anyone's skin, a word of God that doesn't touch the real sin of the society in which it is being proclaimed – what gospel is that?
>
> When the church hears the cry of the oppressed it cannot but denounce the social structures that give rise to and perpetuate the misery from which the cry arises.[5]

4 Adapted from https://en.wikipedia.org/wiki/First_they_came_ ....
5 www.azquotes.com/author/22135-Oscar_Romero.

🕯 How do you respond to these words of Oscar Romero?
To what extent is your faith community actively involved in working for social justice?

⌘

Romero's words challenge us as institutional Church and as individuals to sing our 'The Lord is here' song far and wide, but to do this we have to engage the media more effectively than we have done to date. Although the idea may be anathema to some, I believe it's time for a serious marketing campaign, a way of letting people see the presence of the followers of Jesus in a host of service agencies and helping contexts.

Part of such a campaign will include using a wide range of media to sing our song, tell our stories and let people know where we stand on issues of significance – always emphasizing what connects us with others, the common search for love and meaning, the hope that is to be found in Jesus. Christians are engaged in all sorts of God-inspired work around the globe about which the general public knows little. Even when we are part of a faith community, we often don't know what God is up to in our own regions or down the street. Without this broader perspective, it's easy for us to become discouraged, even fearful for the future of the Church and of the world.

Much work done by Christians is not identified as such by those receiving or witnessing it. When I think about religious 'brand recognition', I think of the Salvation Army with their red shield logo and simple uniform, Buddhist monks in their orange robes, devout Jewish men with their yarmulkes (skull caps) or women with their headscarves. In these examples, the wearing of some recognizable symbol helps to signal the presence of someone who professes their faith in a particular way. Yet the cross, precious and unique to Christianity, has been commandeered for use in personal adornment or as a marker for fatalities, totally separated from the original symbolism. In the past we know that Christianity has used other symbols – the fish for example – to help connect people with the faith, but maybe it's time for us *to reclaim the cross* as our own, and to build a practice of wearing it in some way – on a name-badge, as a necklace, brooch, on a wristband or cap, even as a tattoo – so we can recognize each other beyond the church and so people gradually come to realize how many Christians are at work to help those on the margins.

There will be people in our networks who have advertising and marketing experience and skills – and who want to be part of a push to promote the gospel in ways that counteract the negativity or misinformation prevalent in media reports. We need Christian communicators because reporting on Christian activities can pose problems even for sympathetic media, as Peter Harris comments in relation to environmental action:

> Christian media often fail to make the connection between the mission of the gospel and environmental issues, and give them little attention. Secular media, on the other hand, that are used to covering environmental activists are confused by the wider and more holistic agenda of many Christian groups. They have never encountered people, motivated by faith, who combine a concern for animals and social justice, or for environmental and economic health.[6]

What's your experience of dealing with the media in your area about issues related to matters of faith?
Apart from walking and listening, how do you currently communicate with those in your neighbourhood?

We need all the help we can get in navigating the maze of twenty-first-century communication options. There can be no doubt that if we do not make the most of what technology offers, we will miss chances to share the gospel with those for whom social media, rightly or wrongly, are key sources of experience, connection, information and validation. As Jan Butter, the former Director for Communication of the Anglican Communion, commented:

> Perhaps the biggest threat to spiritual well-being is when human beings choose to seek affirmation and 'love' only online ...

6 http://blog.arocha.org/en/why-conservation-is-a-gospel-issue.

> Having a decent website filled with podcast sermons is a start, but it's simply not enough. When our children are living and dying online shouldn't God's people be on Tumblr, Facebook, and Bebo telling people gathered there that Jesus Christ is the hope of the world who meets all our deepest needs and loves us for who we are?[7]

There are many examples of internet-based opportunities for prayer, such as the Jesuit websites 'Pray as you Go' or 'Sacred Space'[8] both of which provide 10–15-minute scriptural reflections perfect for coffee breaks or travelling on the tube or bus; the North American Society of St John the Evangelist, which invites people to share online a special word or image in preparation for Advent and Lent each year;[9] and the 24–7 prayer movement, a Spirit-led initiative spread by social media. Beginning in the UK with a passionate prayer written on the wall of a prayer room, 24–7 has spread across denominations and continents, maintaining its commitment to pray non-stop. Of this initiative Archbishop Justin Welby has commented:

> I am more and more convinced of the centrality of 24–7 prayer to God's work. It chimes with the spirit of the age. We are at God's moment, all the idols have fallen, and the task is to bring people face to face with Jesus. 24–7 does that for many.[10]

So for those of you who, like me, are bemused by much of social media, the question might be, 'How might we begin to build our capacity to engage in the social media initiatives the Spirit brings to our context?'

Big sigh of relief! A path through the digital maze is offered by Meredith Gould in her book, *The Social Media Gospel: Sharing the Good News in New Ways*. Gould considers that 'today's mission field is online' and walks novices through the process

7 Jan Butter, quoted from her paper, 'Being Human in the Digital Age – an Anglican Perspective', on the Anglican News Service, 14 January 2014.

8 www.pray-as-you-go.org/ (with music) and www.sacredspace.ie.

9 www.ssje.org.

10 www.24-7prayer.com/about.

of coming to grips with using social media as tools for mission, including deciphering the relative usefulness and application of such diverse platforms as Twitter, Instagram, Facebook, podcasts, live-streaming and blogging. She covers tricky questions such as whether 'virtual' community has the same value as 'real' community, firmly states that contact via social media *cannot* replace face-to-face pastoral care, and values *both* print *and* digital media. Gould encourages us to think generationally[11] as we discern how, what, where and when to use social media, and believes that social media can be used to demonstrate how followers of Jesus live. Here's her update on Teresa of Avila's text:

> Christ has no online presence but yours,
> No blog, no Facebook page but yours,
> Yours are the tweets through which love touches this world,
> Yours are the posts through which the Gospel is shared,
> Yours are the updates through which hope is revealed.
> Christ has no online presence but yours,
> No blog, no Facebook page but yours.[12]

Gould also reinforces the value of social media in helping us reach special segments of the community, such as those who have visible or invisible disabilities and people with particular social and spiritual needs, for example immigrants, the elderly or the housebound.[13] It's clear that if we ignore social media, we will be doing a disservice both to those within our church walls for whom digital platforms are becoming increasingly helpful and to those people beyond the Church who have yet to encounter the loving mercy of God, in a language that is familiar.

⌘

11 Meredith Gould, *The Social Media Gospel: Sharing the Good News in New Ways*, 2nd edn, Liturgical Press, Collegeville, MN, 2015; eBook location 424 (Kindle). Gould is referring to the terms 'Silent Generation', 'Baby boomers', Gen X, Millennials and so on.

12 Gould, *The Social Media Gospel*, eBook location 307 (Kindle). (See www.youtube.com/watch?v=Qx-fsRe_ZGo.)

13 Gould, *The Social Media Gospel*, eBook location 957 (Kindle).

Going Deeper: Standing Up and Speaking Out

- What examples of art, sculpture, music or poetry have significantly shaped your faith?

- Whom do you respect as a champion for social justice, environmental action and so on?
  How would you rate your own participation in such action to date? Talk to God about your response.

- Consider your own experience of using social media, for example by writing a blog, posting on Facebook.
  How have you found this experience?
  What are the blessings and the pitfalls?

- Explore the websites of your neighbouring churches, the local diocese and an international agency such as Amnesty International or Oxfam. Note what appeals, repels, might be relevant in your context.
  How might you upgrade/make a website for your own congregation and what might go on that site?

Costly loving

> Whoever comes to me and does not hate father and mother, wife and children, brothers and sisters, yes, and even life itself, cannot be my disciple. Whoever does not carry the cross and follow me cannot be my disciple. For which of you, intending to build a tower, does not first sit down and estimate the cost, to see whether he has enough to complete it?
>
> *Luke 14.26–28*

Bishop Tom Wright in his clarification of this troubling passage comments that:

> Jesus is not denying the importance of close family and the propriety of living in supportive harmony with them. But when there is an urgent task to be done, as there now is, then everything else, including one's own life, must be put at risk for the sake of the kingdom …
>
> The same is true of possessions. Many of Jesus' followers, then and now, have owned houses and lands, and have not felt compelled to abandon them. But being prepared to do so is the sign that one has understood the seriousness of the call to follow Jesus.[1]

Following the Way of Jesus is no walk in the park. Those who think that Christianity is a prop for the weak, haven't considered the challenges of spiritual growth, nor do they know the stories of people who, in Jesus' name, have set aside personal ambition

1 Tom Wright, *Luke for Everyone*, SPCK, London, 2001, pp. 180–1.

to serve the less fortunate, have worked in difficult conditions to bring hope and healing, even been martyred as they performed deeds of mercy. While few of us will experience that ultimate cost of discipleship, following Jesus into the community can mean a review of our priorities or a totally unexpected call:

> A Board member of a Christian care home contacted me to see if I knew of anyone interested in being their new chaplain as they were struggling to fill the position. I agreed to pray about it but when I rang back it was with the awkward admission, 'I'm sorry – the only name that kept coming up was my own!' The call was confirmed by the Board's rapid, affirming response.
>
> This new ministry was unexpected, even unwanted, but God showed me that I was to keep the residents company in their vulnerability, love them as far as I was able and ease their dying. And they would teach me to share more of who I really was and to believe that I was lovable. And so it was.
>
> I loved and served them for almost six years, until I became exhausted from the deaths and diminishment, and the constant availability, and chose to retire, so someone else could give them the care they deserved.

Has there been a time in your life or ministry when you have had to pull back from something you really loved because you simply could not continue?
What was that like for you? What support did you have?
How have you supported someone else facing burnout, exhaustion or transition?

Jesus reminded his followers to be prepared to leave everything for him. Once we are seriously receptive to partnering God beyond the Church, we will find that, as we increasingly align ourselves with the countercultural values and practices of Jesus the servant, there will be a price to pay. It will cost us:

- to go beyond our comfort zones, beyond the familiar church culture into the neighbourhood

- to get close to people – to care deeply, witness their pain, pray with them, advocate for them
- to re-present a religion that has so much 'bad press'
- to risk challenge, even opposition, from within our families or among our friends
- to allow God to strip us of all that bolsters our ego and gives us false security
- not to know the way ahead – to 'make the road by walking'[2]
- to identify with a community that is deprived of adequate resources for healthy living
- to become part of public action to remediate injustice or violence.

🕯 How do these 'costs' relate to your own life?
What other 'costs' of discipleship are you already aware of from your experience?

Giving up what makes us feel secure is a critical dynamic of the journey of faith. We are called to grow in trust into the full stature of Christ,[3] and to do that we have to be prepared to let go of everything on which we've built our public self and carefully protected well-being, so our true, Christ-self can flourish. It is the way of downward mobility, of unknowing, of vulnerability and seeming powerlessness. Not surprisingly, many of us resist, trying to hold on to what we've always done the way we've always done it, mistakenly placing our trust and shoring up our identity in routines and ritual, roles and status, rather than in who we are in Christ.

One who didn't resist was Mark Beale[4] who, with his wife Barbara, was given the task of establishing a church and vicarage in a muddy field in South Auckland in 1988. As a 19 year old, Beale had given his life to Christ and, as he made his commitment prayer, the whole room lit up and he began to speak in tongues.

---

2 Brian McLaren, *We Make the Road by Walking*, Jericho Books, New York, 2014.

3 Ephesians 4.13.

4 www.listener.co.nz/currently/social-issues/vicar-mark-beale-sharing-the-cake.

He couldn't understand it or rationalize it, but it set him on the Way, and by the time he came to South Auckland he had become sure of who he was in Christ.

Until retirement in 2016, this couple and their family were embedded in their community: honouring God's presence; their children attending local schools; building relationships; critiquing government policies; offering remedial education, advocacy services and restorative justice; working for affordable housing, starting projects to improve the local environment and always affirming the goodness of the community. In that time they've been burgled, verbally abused, got used to being let down and have had to watch the deadly upward spiral of rents and housing prices wreak havoc on the people and the community they loved. At 65, Mark knew it was time for someone with more energy to minister to the 250 people who now attend St Elizabeth's. He plans to do more work with those in prison and on release, to help them make a fresh start.

How does this example of costly loving resonate with your own experience?
What questions does it raise?

It cost Jesus everything to take the path of surrender and resolute trust, to empty himself of Trinitarian relationship, of cosmic connection and take on earthy flesh. It's impossible for us even to glimpse what this kenosis[5] was like for him, when we have such a difficult time 'dying to self', letting our ego shift from centre stage so we can become open enough for the Spirit to work in and through us.

Some have attempted to put words around their experience of being fully open – however fleetingly – to God's life in them. The fourteenth-century Persian poet Hafiz is purported to have written of himself:

5 Becoming entirely receptive to God's divine will.

I am
a hole in a flute
that the Christ's breath
moves through
–
listen to this
music.[6]

7

In the late 1800s, St Thérès of Lisieux described herself as 'a ball in the hands of the child Jesus'; and Mother Teresa, now formally St Teresa of Calcutta, described herself as 'a pencil in God's hands'.[8]

🕯 Take a moment to reflect on these three metaphors. What do they have in common?

What figure of speech might you choose to describe your own life surrendered to Christ?

With the publication of Mother Teresa's correspondence with her confessors, we've been given a unique insight into costly loving. In her earlier years as a vowed religious, she had been blessed with an awareness of Christ's love in unmistakable experiences of grace. But when she began to work among the poor and dying on the streets, the felt experience of the Jesus, whom she loved like no other, left her. Instead she felt emptiness, what spiritual directors know as a 'dark night of the soul'. This intensification of longing for more of God, coupled with a profound sense of God's absence, persisted for decades. Although some considered this sense of absence to be a loss of faith, a discerning spiritual adviser, Revd Joseph Neuner, assured her that:

> there was no human remedy for it (that is, she should not feel responsible for affecting it); that feeling Jesus is not the only proof of his being there, and her very craving for God was

6 *Love poems from God: 12 Sacred Voices from East and West*, trans. Daniel Ladinsky, Penguin, New York, 2002, p. 153.

7 From mayaningunlugu.blogspot.com, 'Playing the Persian nev'.

8 Mother Teresa, *A Simple Path*, complied by Lucinda Varley, Random House, New York, 1995.

> a 'sure sign' of his 'hidden presence' in her life; and that the absence was in fact part of the 'spiritual side' of her work for Jesus.

Teresa had desired to share Christ's passion, but had not expected to get close to Jesus' felt experience of the absence of God when he was on the cross. As David van Biema writes:

> The idea that rather than a nihilistic vacuum, his felt absence might be the ordeal she had prayed for, that her perseverance in its face might echo his faith unto death on the Cross, that it might indeed be a grace, enhancing the efficacy of her calling, made sense of her pain. Neuner would later write, 'It was the redeeming experience of her life when she realized that the night of her heart was the special share she had in Jesus' passion.'[9]

Whatever shape our venture into the neighbourhood takes, we are assured that the Spirit will lead us if we are attentive and faithful to Jesus and if we remember that we do not walk this path alone.

⌘

Going Deeper: Costly Loving

- How aware are you of your own/your congregation's resistance to God's invitation to follow Jesus into the community?
- How might you work with this resistance and find a way forward?
- What is your own experience of a 'felt absence of God' – what St John of the Cross called the 'dark night of the soul'?
- Meditate on Psalm 139.11–12, 'even the darkness is as light to you'.

9 David van Biema, 'Mother Teresa's Crisis of Faith', *Time Magazine*, 23 August 2007.

Reflect on a time when God led you into something you thought you couldn't handle.
What happened?
How might this inform your willingness to follow Jesus into the unknown, 'to make the path by walking'?

Continuing the story …

I hesitate to write about *how* what you've read and explored in this book might be used in your local context. *Only* the Holy Spirit will know how best to support your continuing spiritual formation as disciples of Jesus and your practical application as witnesses; *Only* the Holy Spirit can help you sing your God-song as you join the divine presence in your particular neighbourhood.

So what follows is tentative, invitational. May some of it ring true with you and/or spark further divine discoveries about what God has in mind for you and your people as you apply this material in faith and trust.

- Once you've integrated the material personally, work through it again with your ministry team/colleagues/those whom the Spirit brings to mind. Then you can discern together how God might want to help you best use this resource in your context, such as sermon series on 'God-spotting', workshops on 'spiritual conversation', small-group focus on 'Listening', opportunities to share God-stories, parish or group commitment to intentional discipleship and witness.
- In your context this material may serve as a follow-up to ALPHA – people newly opened to the Holy Spirit may well value the chance to hone their 'listening to God' skills with a view to being able to share their recently enlivened God-songs with others. Ongoing discipling would have a focus and energy about it because it is being linked to real-time mission beyond the doors of the church.
- Be alert for how you might incorporate some of this material into existing small-group meetings, such as AAW/Mothers' Union, Vestry, Study groups.

- Consider using this book in the early stages of any Mission Action Planning;[1] that is, before doing the community audit. Information gained through census data or mapping locations of key features such as schools, offices, parks, community facilities tells us only so much. Equipping the congregation to go out into their communities to discover 'on the ground' what's going on will yield living information and build connections.[2]
- As a way to encourage people's participation, consider setting up and supporting PowerPods – pairs or trios who can work through the material, practise listening to each other and encourage each other to try spiritual conversation in their own neighbourhood and be on the alert for the spiritual needs of those they meet.
- Several PowerPods could meet for a monthly Formation Forum during which teaching, discussion, planning and prayer would allow participants to receive support and enrichment.
- Consider doing your own version of the story project undertaken by St Paul's in Auckland – imagine providing a context for God-songs to be shared and for your people to see how active and practical God is. Not only would they be drawn closer to God but also to each other, *and* they would get valuable practice in singing their God-songs before heading off into the neighbourhood!
- Alternatively, on a smaller scale, invite parishioners to tell their story through the church magazine, website or a special slot in regular services.
- Actively seek funding for someone to work with you as a parish/diocese to help you all build capacity to listen and witness.
- Make it standard practice to begin meetings with an opportunity to share God-moments with each other – ten minutes in pairs – with time for whole group sharing if anyone wishes ☺

1 Philip Giddings, Chair of the Mission and Public Affairs Council, *Mission Action Planning in the Church of England: Briefing Note from the Mission and Public Affairs Council*, June 2011; www.churchofengland.org/media/1281665/gs%201835b.pdf.

2 Visit www.stalbans.anglican.org/faith/map-planning for a useful diagram, which shows engagement with the community as the first step on the prayer-centred journey to effective mission.

- Consider what makes your context unique and focus on that special character. For example, the Diocese of St Asaph in North Wales recognized the decline in the storytelling tradition in Wales and has engaged the services of experienced youth-worker and storyteller, Mark Yaconelli as Missioner in Residence. This is an intentional move with substantial funding behind it 'as a way of encouraging churchgoers to tell their story – and the story of God's work in their lives, in what has been dubbed "the Gospel according to everybody"'. Yaconelli emphasizes that what has to happen first is *listening* to the community, and *listening* to others people's stories before sharing our own.[3]

⌘

In Disney's 2015 film *Cinderella*, Ella's dying mother gives her daughter words to last a lifetime: 'Have courage. Be kind.' And Ella does just that, in spite of shabby treatment until she meets her prince.

What words from Jesus would I want to leave with you?

> 'Do not be afraid.' (Matthew 10.31; John 6.20)
> 'Let me give you a new command: Love one another. In the same way I loved you, you love one another. This is how everyone will recognize that you are my disciples – when they see the love you have for each other.' (John 13.34–35, *The Message*)

And when we are bogged down or anxious about the Church, the beloved Bride of Christ, let's remember that God is creative and faithful, and *is* breathing new life into worn and weary minds all over the world. Let's keep our focus on singing the love song God has formed in our lives – a song shaped by suffering, but transformed by knowing God's love is with us, for all people, for ever.

My hope and prayer is that this resource will be taken and broken open and spread with joy by those who follow Jesus, that

3 'The Gospel According to Everybody', posted on the Anglican News Service on 25 February 2016. Available at www.anglicannews.org/features/2016/02/the-gospel-according-to-everybody.aspx.

God may be glorified and the Spirit be released to help us sing our God-song wherever we find ourselves. With confidence in Christ, and by our prayerful and loving presence, may we proclaim that 'The Lord is here! God's Spirit is indeed with us.'

THE LORD IS HERE[4]

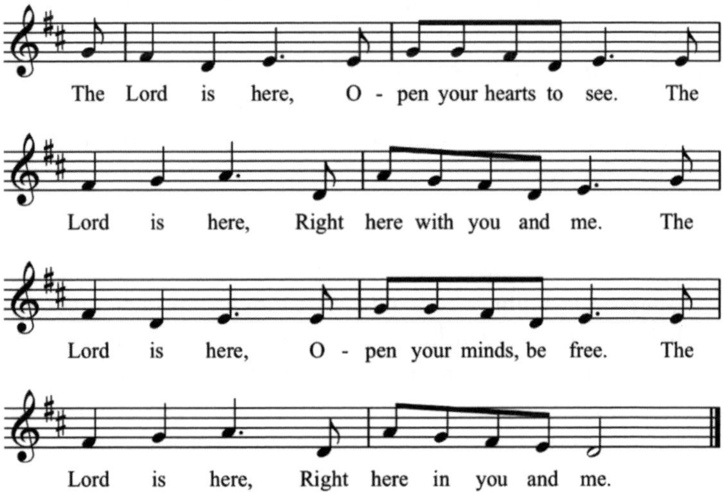
The Lord is here, O - pen your hearts to see. The
Lord is here, Right here with you and me. The
Lord is here, O - pen your minds, be free. The
Lord is here, Right here in you and me.

4 Feel free to add verses by substituting 'Jesus', 'Creator God' or 'The Holy One' for 'The Lord' as fits your context – enjoy!

Further reading

Part 1

Indwell the Gospels

Adam, David, *The Rhythm of Life*, 2nd edn, Church House Publishing, London, 2007 (daily office for seven days).

—— *Tides and Seasons: Modern Prayers in the Celtic Tradition*, SPCK, London, 2010.

—— *The Edge of Glory*, SPCK, London, 2011.

Aisthorpe, Steve, *The Invisible Church: Learning from the Experiences of Churchless Christians*, St Andrew Press, Edinburgh, 2016.

Benner, David, *The Gift of Being Yourself*, Inter-Varsity [illegible] Downers Grove, IL, 2004.

Bourgeault, Cynthia, *Centring Prayer and Inner Awakening*, Cowley Publications, Cambridge, MA, 2004.

Brother Lawrence, *Practising the Presence of God*, various editions.

Darragh, Neil (ed.), *Living in the Planet Earth: Faith Communities and Ecology*, Accent, Auckland, NZ, 2016.

Fowler, James, *Stages of Faith: The Psychology of Human Development and the Quest for Meaning*, HarperOne, New York, 1995.

Freeman, Laurence, *Sensing God: Learning to Meditate Through Lent*, SPCK, London, 2015; or watch him speaking on www.youtube.com/watch?v=SkJ_y1b204A.

Guenther, Margaret, *Holy Listening: The Art of Spiritual Direction*, Cowley Publications, Cambridge, MA, 1992.

Harris, Peter, *Under the Bright Wings*, Regent College Publishing, Vancouver, 2000. The story of the first ten years of A Rocha.

—— *Kingfisher's Fire: A Story of Hope for God's Earth*, Monarch Books, Oxford, 2008.

Hedahl, Susan K., *Listening Ministry: Rethinking Pastoral Leadership*, Augsburg Fortress, Minneapolis, MN, 2002.

Hopkins, Gerald Manley, e.g. 'Pied Beauty', 'As Kingfishers Catch Fire', collected works available in many editions.

Jamieson, Alan, *Called Again in and Beyond the Deserts of Faith*, Philip Garside, Wellington, NZ, 2004.

—— *Chrysalis: The Hidden Transformation in the Journey of Faith*, Authentic Media/Paternoster, Milton Keynes, 2007.

Jamieson, Alan, J. McIntosh and A. Thompson, *Five Years On*, Portland Research Trust, Wellington, NZ, 2006.

Keating, Thomas, *Intimacy with God*, Crossroad, New York, 2004.

Linn, Dennis, Sheila Fabricant Linn and Matthew Linn, *Sleeping with Bread: Holding what Gives you Life*, Paulist Press, New York, 1995. An accessible exploration of the practice of the examen.

Maden, Bruce, *God is in the Neighbourhood*, Spiritual Growth Ministries, Aotearoa, NZ, 2006. Available for download at www.sgm.org.nz/research_papers.htm.

Newbigin, Lesslie, *Foolishness to the Greeks: The Gospel and Western Culture*, Eerdmans, Grand Rapids, MI, 1986.

—— *The Gospel in a Pluralist Society*, Eerdmans, Grand Rapids, MI, 1989.

O'Donohue, John, *Anam Cara: A Book of Celtic Wisdom*, HarperCollins, New York, 1997.

Oliver, Mary, e.g. 'Praying' in *Thirst*, Beacon Press, Boston, 2006, and see www.youtube.com/watch?v=ETIxcnfOsWw.

Pickering, Sue, *Spiritual Direction: A Practical Introduction*, Canterbury Press, Norwich, 2008.

Rohr, Richard, *Contemplation in Action*, Crossroad, New York, 2006.

Ryan, Thomas, *Interreligious Prayer: A Christian Guide*, Paulist Press, Mahwah, NJ, 2008.

Saint Teresa of Avila, *The Interior Castle*, various editions.

Slee, Nicola, *Women's Faith Development: Patterns and Processes*, Routledge, Oxford, 2004.

Websites

A Rocha – Christian conservation group: www.arocha.org/en (then search for the link to your country's A Rocha website).

The Bishop's Action Foundation website: www.bishopsaction foundation.org.nz/page/the-beginning-of-the-story/4/16.

The Carmelites who have a long association with *lectio divina*: http://ocarm.org/en/content/lectio.

The two main advocates of Christian contemplative prayer:
Contemplative Outreach: www.contemplativeoutreach.org/category/category/centering-prayer (Thomas Keating, Cynthia Bourgeault).
The World Community of Christian meditation: www.wccm.org (Laurence Freeman).

The Church of the Saviour, Washington, DC: http://inwardout ward.org/the-church-of-the-saviour/our-story.

The Community of St Anselm, 'devoted to prayer and serving the poor': Lambeth Palace, London – www.stanselm.org.uk.

The Contemplative Fire dispersed community: www.contemplative fire.org/index.htm.

Explorefaith.org – providing resources for spiritual growth – this particular post looks at 'thin places': www.explorefaith.org/mystery/mysteryThinPlaces.html.

The International Community of Aidan and Hilda – www.ray simpson.org.

The Magdalene and Thistle House communities have emerged in response to a need to support women transitioning out of prostitution in the USA. A video about their early work is embedded in Karyn Wiseman's blog: www.huffingtonpost.com/karyn-l-wiseman-phd/finding-light-in-the-dark-hope-inside-desperate-discourse-john-21-1-19_b_9611412.html, or visit http://episcopaldigitalnetwork.com/ens/2013/10/16/from-5-women-in-a-nashville-home-to-a-nationwide-movement.

Mindmapping:
Go to http://mindmapfree.com/# for a free tool to help you visualize and organize your information into a flexible diagram.

The Missional Network – Alan Roxburgh and team: http://the missionalnetwork.com/category.

Te Aroha Noa, Palmerston North, NZ, 'Working alongside whanau (extended family) to create change': www.tearohanoa.org.nz.

Part 2

Indwell the Acts of the Apostles

Anglican News Service, *The Gospel According to Everybody*, posted 25 February 2016. Available at www.anglicannews.org/features/2016/02/the-gospel-according-to-everybody.aspx.

Blue, Ken, *Healing Spiritual Abuse: How to Break Free from Bad Church Experiences*, Inter-Varsity Press, Downers Grove, IL, 1993.

Chester, Tim and Steve Timmis, *Everyday Church: Mission by being Good Neighbours*, Inter-Varsity Press, Downers Grove, IL, 2011.

Greig, Peter and Dave Roberts, *Red Moon Rising: How 24-7 Prayer Is Awakening a Generation*, Kingsway, Eastbourne, 2003.

Lentz, Robert and Edwina Gately, *Christ in the Margins*, Orbis Books, Maryknoll, NY, 2003.

McLaren, Brian D., *A Generous Orthodoxy*, Zondervan, Grand Rapids, MI, 2004.

—— *We Make the Road by Walking*, Jericho Books, New York, 2014.

—— *The Great Spiritual Migration: How the World's Largest Religion is Seeking a Better Way to be Christian*, Convergent Books, Penguin/Random House, New York, 2016.

Newell, John Philip, *The Rebirthing of God: Christianity's Struggle for New Beginnings*, Skylight Paths, Vermont, 2014.

Pickering, Sue, *Creative Ideas for Ministry with the Aged*, Canterbury Press, Norwich, 2014.

Randerson, Richard, *Slipping the Moorings*, Matai House, Wellington, NZ, 2015.

Rupp, Joyce, *Little Pieces of Light: Darkness and Personal Growth*, Illuminations, Grand Rapids, MI, 1994.

Swinton, John and Richard Payne, *Living Well and Dying Faith-*

fully: Christian Practices for End-of-Life Care, Eerdmans, Grand Rapids, MI, 2009.

Taylor, Steve, *The Out of Bounds Church? Learning to Create a Community of Faith in a Culture of Change*, Zondervan, Grand Rapids, MI, 2005.

Websites

Anglican Marks of Mission – see www.anglicancommunion.org/identity/marks-of-mission.aspx.

Apologetics – for reasoned defences of the faith and discussion about contemporary issues see:
The Oxford Centre for Christian Apologetics: http://theocca.org.occa.
The C. S. Lewis Society: www.apologetics.org.

Mark Beale – for the full text of the article, visit www.listener.co.nz/current-affairs/social-issues-current-affairs/sharing-the-cake.

Conservation – http://blog.arocha.org/en/why-conservation-is-a-gospel-issue.

Dysfunctional triangulation: originally addressed by Murray Bowen in his Family Systems Theory – see www.youtube.com/watch?v=47rDdeSPTGs.

The human spirit in the face of tragedy: Antoine Leiris, widowed in the Paris Bataclan massacre: www.theguardian.com/world/2015/nov/17/bataclan-paris-victim-helene-muyal-husband-antoine-leiris-killers-open-letter.

Alana Levandoski's recent album *Behold, I Make all Things New* is a 'Christ Narrative', complemented by a book of lyrics and original art. See https://alanalevandoski.com.

The Liturgists – for creative liturgy, art, music and podcasts. See www.theliturgists.com.

Mission action planning – www.stalbans.anglican.org/faith/map-planning – a useful diagram shows engagement with the community as the first step on the prayer-centred journey to effective mission.

Orlando shooting report: see CNN interview with Shane Tomlinson's parents: http://edition.cnn.com/videos/us/2016/06/17/

shane-tomlinson-parents-remember-their-son-sot-lemon-tonight.cnn/video/playlists/who-are-the-orlando-shooting-victims.

Restorative Justice – see www.rpiassn.org/practice-areas/what-is-restorative-justice.

24/7 Prayer initiative – see www.24-7prayer.com/story#/24-7story/prayer-explosion.

Bibliography

A New Zealand Prayer Book, Collins, London, 1989.

Badham, Paul, 'Religion in Britain and China: Similarities and Differences', in *Modern Believing* 49:1, January 2008.

Barrett Browning, Elizabeth, *Aurora Leigh*, 1856, at www.bartleby.com/236/86.html.

Bonhoeffer, Dietrich, *The Cost of Discipleship*, SCM Press, Norwich, anniversary edition, 2015. First published in 1937.

Bowler, James M., 'SHAME: A Primary Root of Resistance to Movement in Direction', in *PRESENCE: The Journal of Spiritual Directors International* 3:3, September 1997.

Brueggemann, Walter, *Spirituality of the Psalms*, Fortress Press: Minneapolis, MN, 2002.

Claiborne, Shane and Tony Campolo, *Red Letter Revolution: What if Jesus Really Meant What he Said?*, Thomas Nelson, Nashville, TN, 2012.

De Waal, Esther, *The Celtic Way of Prayer*, Hodder & Stoughton, London, 1996.

Ebaugh, H. R. F., *Becoming an EX: The Process of Role Exit*, University of Chicago Press, Chicago, 1988.

Education for Ministry website: http://efm.sewanee.edu; UK website www.efmuk.org.uk.

Francis, James Allan, *One Solitary Life*, widely available online. Originally published in the author's *The Real Jesus and Other Sermons*, The Judson Press, Philadelphia, 1926.

Giddings, Philip, *Mission Action Planning in the Church of England: Briefing Note from the Mission and Public Affairs Council*, June 2011; see www.churchofengland.org/media/1281665/gs%201835b.pdf.

Gould, Meredith, *The Social Media Gospel: Sharing the Good News in New Ways*, 2nd edn, Liturgical Press, Collegeville, MN, 2015.

Grant, Esther (managing ed.), *St Paul's Stories*, St Paul's Anglican Church, Auckland, NZ, 2015.

Harris, Peter, *A Report from the World Conservation Congress, 1–10 September 2016*. First published on *Christianity Today*, 8 September.

Hay, David, *The Spirituality of the Unchurched*, conference paper, British and Irish Mission Association, 2000 from research undertaken by D. Hay and K. Hunt K., *Understanding the Spirituality of People Who Don't go to Church*, Centre for the Study of Human Relations, University of Nottingham, 2000.

Jamieson, Alan, *A Churchless Faith: Faith Journeys beyond the Churches*, SPCK, London, 2002.

Kafwanka, John and Mark Oxbrow (eds), *Intentional Discipleship and Disciple-making: An Anglican Guide for Christian Life and Formation*, Anglican Consultative Council, London, 2016.

Keating, Thomas, *Invitation to Love: The Way of Christian Contemplation*, Continuum, New York, 1995.

Kidd, Sue Monk, *When the Heart Waits*, Harper & Row, San Francisco, 1992.

Killen, Patricia O'Connell and John de Beer, *The Art of Theological Reflection*, Crossroad, New York, 2002.

Koenig, Harold G., *Spirituality in Patient Care*, 2nd edn, Templeton Foundation Press, London, 2007.

Ladinsky, Daniel (trans.), *Love Poems from God: 12 Sacred Voices from East and West*, Penguin, New York, 2002.

Lowney, Chris, *Pope Francis: Why he Leads the Way he Leads*, Loyola Press, Chicago, 2013.

MacKinlay, Elizabeth, *Spiritual Growth and Care in the Fourth Age of Life*, Jessica Kingsley Publishers, London, 2006.

May, Gerald, *Care of Mind, Care of Spirit*, HarperCollins, New York, 1992.

—— *The Dark Night of the Soul: A Psychiatrist Explores the Connection Between Darkness and Spiritual Growth*, Harper & Row, San Francisco, 2005.

Miles, Sara, *Take this Bread: A Radical Conversion*, Canterbury Press, Norwich, 2012.

Mother Teresa, *Come be My Light*, ed. Brian Kolodiejchuk, Rider, London, 2009.

Newberg, Andrew, Eugene D'Aquili and Vince Rause, *Why God Won't Go Away: Brain Science and the Biology of Belief*, Ballantine Books, New York, 2001.

Parsons, Melissa, *Rubble to Resurrection: Churches respond in the Canterbury Quakes*, Daystar, Auckland, NZ, 2014.

Pearce, David, *Kondoa 31: One Man's Journey through Life*, self-published, 2015.

Pritchard, John, *How to Explain your Faith*, SPCK, London, 2006.

—— *God Lost and Found*, SPCK, London, 2011.

—— *Living Faithfully*, SPCK, London, 2013.

Randerson, Richard, *Engagement 21: A Wake-up Call to the 21st Century Church in Mission*, Matai House: Wellington, NZ, 2010, available free as a pdf from randersonjr@paradise.net.nz.

Roxburgh, Alan, *Missional: Joining God in the Neighborhood*, Baker Books, Grand Rapids, MI, 2011.

—— *Joining God, Remaking Church, Changing the World*, Morehouse, New York, 2015.

Trokan, John, 'Models of Theological Reflection (1997)', in *Journal of Inquiry and Practice* 1:2, July 2013.

van Biema, David, 'Mother Teresa's crisis of Faith', in *Time Magazine*, 23 August 2007.

Index of names and subjects